Myth, Reality, and Reform

Higher Education Policy in Latin America

Claudio de Moura Castro and Daniel C. Levy

Distributed by The Johns Hopkins University Press
for the Inter-American Development Bank

Washington, D.C.
2000

©2000 Inter-American Development Bank
1300 New York Avenue, N.W.
Washington, D.C. 20577

Cover: Images © 2000 PhotoDisc, Inc.

Produced by the IDB Publications Section. Views and opinions expressed in this publication are those of the authors and do not necessarily reflect the official positions of the Inter-American Development Bank.

To order this book, contact
IDB Bookstore
idb-books@iadb.org
www.iadb.org/pub
Tel: (202) 623-1753; Fax: (202) 623-1709
1-877-782-7432

Cataloging-in-Publication data provided by the
Inter-American Development Bank
Felipe Herrera Library

Castro, Claudio de Moura.
   Myth, reality, and reform : higher education policy in Latin America
/ Claudio de Moura Castro and Daniel C. Levy.

        p. cm.
        Includes bibliographical references.
        ISBN: 1886938601

        1.Education, Higher—Latin America. 2.Educational change—Latin
America. 3.Education and state—Latin America. I. Levy, Daniel C.
II. Inter-American Development Bank. III. Title.

338.9 I573—dc21

Library of Congress Control Number: 00-131225

CONTENTS

FOREWORD

Higher education plays a crucial role in the development and leadership of Latin America and the Caribbean, and in today's world of fast-increasing diversification, which requires an array of educational options.

Higher education, once reserved for preparing the elite, long ago moved into the professional areas. It provides the general education that people need as citizens and workers, and technical training for highly skilled workers in modern economies. Higher education is being called on to fulfill a variety of roles and to deal with formidable differentiation in the background of students, scholastic ability, labor markets, and social roles. These conditions present a challenge to today's policymakers.

The region's system of higher education has many strengths and examples of excellence. At the same time, however, waste, inefficiency, and chronic distortions remain serious and endemic problems. Governance is poor in most public institutions and rules and regulations do not provide the appropriate incentives.

Myth, Reality, and Reform tries to make sense of the dynamics in higher education in Latin America and the Caribbean, examining institutions, rules, incentives, and functions. Since Felipe Herrera, the IDB's first president, said that this was the "bank of education," the Bank has confronted these topical issues, most recently with the formulation of its Higher Education Strategy. It is our hope that this book will contribute to these current discussions and help build a new consensus on higher education in the region.

Waldemar W. Wirsig
Manager, Sustainable Development Department
Inter-American Development Bank

CHAPTER 1

INTRODUCTION

Two debilitating tendencies dominate assessments of the state of higher education in Latin America. One, a common perspective within the region's universities, minimizes the deficiencies and the need for major change. The other, a common critique disseminated by governments and international financial institutions, bashes the system and seeks change through the introduction of sometimes alien policies.[1] Instead, this book suggests how governments and institutions can bolster existing positive features while fundamentally reforming weaker features.

Our proper subject of discussion is higher education, which is also called post-secondary education or tertiary education (OECD 1998a). A central point in the assessment is that higher education in the region is very diverse. Not just performance but functions themselves vary across nations, sectors, institutions, and units within institutions. We identify patterns of success and failure by distinguishing between the real and perceived functions undertaken.

We analyze Latin American higher education in terms of four major functions: academic leadership, professional development, technological training and development, and general higher education. The last function, which can be the most vexing, requires an initial explanation. This type of post-secondary education typically claims to provide a professional curriculum and method of instruction. In reality, it offers "quasi-professional" or general education. For the most part, it produces graduates who do not find employment directly corresponding to their fields of study.

---

[1] Harsh criticism has come from Latin American scholars of higher education (as cited, for example, in the section on shortcomings in chapter 2). By contrast, the United Nations Educational, Scientific, and Cultural Organization (UNESCO) and its leading advisors have usually taken a less critical view, citing problems, challenges, and opportunities much more than failings, and framing proposals more in terms of broad goals than specifics (UNESCO 1995; Tunnermann 1996).

Failure to identify the different functions of higher education contributes to sloppy assessment and a lack of appropriate policies. Ironically, it leads to both too little criticism, as institutions hide behind rationales that do not fit them, and excessive criticism, as institutions fail in their ostensible missions even while performing other credible ones. By contrast, proper identification gives a better idea of what works and what does not, and allows policy recommendations to be tailored accordingly. Although our analysis focuses on Latin America, this typology of functions might prove suggestive and adaptable for assessments and policy recommendations in other regions as well.

Fundamentally driving this book is our conviction that higher education policy matters. It would matter simply on the basis of the substantial investment in higher education. In Latin America this includes years in the lives of over seven million students and large public expenditures. (See table 1.1 for enrollment by country and table 1.2 for expenditures on higher education.) Moreover, demography, expanding secondary school enrollments, economic change, and social aspirations indicate that higher education in Latin America will grow considerably in the coming years, soon to ten million students. But higher education policy also matters because it must be linked to development to build more productive, informed, prosperous, just, fulfilling, and democratic societies.

Higher education has played an important role for centuries. Now, more than ever before, the region needs to nurture its human resources through advanced formal education. Latin America's modernization and integration into the global economy and society depends on higher education. We reject the view that higher education can be marginal to national development, or that the state or society can be marginal to higher education.[2] We also reject the view that higher education can play its role well if only it is expanded and nourished with more generous public funds. In other words, as significant size and growth are givens, and as vital tasks must be carried out, it is crucial that close attention be paid to the scope and quality of higher education's performance. In this context, we argue for important additional reforms.

---

[2] In this respect, we remain sympathetic to a rather large literature by Latin American scholars in the 1960s and 1970s, who stressed the importance of higher education in national development. See, for example, Scherz (1975), CPU (1986), Dooner and Lavados (1979), and Atria et al. (1972).

Table 1.1. Enrollment in Higher Education, 1994

Country	Enrollment (thousands)	Population (thousands)	Enrollment rate
Argentina	1,054	2,711	38.9
Bolivia	154	676	22.8
Brazil	1,661	14,508	11.4
Chile	327	1,231	26.6
Colombia	561[a]	3,197	17.6
Costa Rica	84	285	29.3
Cuba	176	1,118	15.8
Dominican Republic	113	747	15.1
Ecuador	213	1,082	19.7
El Salvador	108	565	19.1
Guatemala	113	919	12.3
Honduras	54	507	10.6
Mexico	1,304	9,452	13.8
Nicaragua	42	375	11.2
Panama	70	252	27.6
Paraguay	53	429	12.3
Peru	643	2,274	28.3
Uruguay	75	250	29.9
Venezuela	601	1,915	31.4
Total	7,405	42,493	20.7[b]

a. Data are for 1993.

b. The regional average is a little high because it is a nonweighted average of the country averages.

Source: García Guadilla (1996b:270); CEPAL (1994).

Given the importance of higher education in Latin America, the lack of serious study about it is worrying, although there has been growth in the last decade or two. The only time that higher education commanded great attention within the larger academic fields of Latin American studies or comparative political sociology, for example, was in the 1960s, around the issue of student activism. Within the region, there have been studies over time, but more in terms of essays about what the university should do than about what it actually does.

Table 1.2. The Higher Education Budget, 1994

Country	Year	Total (thousands of dollars)	Percentage of national budget	Percentage of education budget
Argentina	1994	1,651,000	2.2	16.5
Bolivia	1994	77,352	6.1	26.8
Brazil[a]	1994	2,269,420	2.8	35.5
Chile	1994	306,604	2.8	19.1
Colombia	1993	376,000	2.7	20.0
Costa Rica	1994	92,065	4.7	22.2
Cuba	1994	207,700	1.7	15.3
Dominican Rep.		13,771	0.9	10.0
Ecuador	1994	108,000	3.7	21.4
El Salvador	1994	21,600	2.0	12.8
Guatemala	1995	53,651	3.4	28.6
Honduras	1994	27,278	4.1	20.4
Mexico	1994	927,813	2.3	10.4
Nicaragua	1994	26,080	6.3	33.9
Panama	1994	86,171	2.0	22.8
Paraguay[b]	1994	39,725	3.6	19.3
Peru	1993	144,213	2.3	13.8
Uruguay[c]	1995	118,000	3.1	20.4
Venezuela[d]	1994	867,850	6.8	43.6
Total		7,414,293	2.7	20.4

a. Federal budget; no information available on state and municipal budgets.
b. Universidad de la Asunción.
c. Budget of the Universidad de la República, which accounts for the bulk of the higher education budget.
d. University budget.
Source: García Guadilla (1996b:285).

Aided by improvements in national data collection, empirical studies have increased in recent years, usually by scholars from the larger nations. Many of these studies focus on policies. The region needs more in-depth scholarship on almost every aspect of higher education. This research, in turn, would provide a firmer base upon which to analyze policy.

In addition to worthwhile overviews, there are now a few comparative policy analyses (Balán 1999; Kent 1996, 1997; Courard 1993).[3]

Probably the largest research center devoted to higher education studies is the Centro de Estudios sobre la Universidad (CESU) within the Coordinación de Humanidades of Mexico's National University. CESU has produced a large series of books, some on Mexico and some on Latin America more broadly (for example, Esquivel 1995). Another research center of note is the Higher Education Research Group (NUPES) at the Universidade de São Paulo, which produces a valuable series of working papers. Several other social science research centers have included higher education within their scope of study. Prominent examples are FLACSO-Chile, CEDES (Centro de Estudios de Estado y Sociedad) in Argentina, and the Instituto de Estudios Políticos y Relaciones Internacionales de la Universidad Nacional de Colombia. Chile's Corporación Promoción Universitaria (CPU) has produced a significant share of the best work on Latin American higher education for decades.[4] CINDA (Centro Interuniversitario de Desarrollo) is another Santiago-based center that has produced studies on Latin American higher education. CRESALC (Centro Regional para la Educacion Superior en America Latina y el Caribe) has been important in recent years, especially for its compilation of data. Located in Caracas, CRESALC is the Latin American wing of the United Nations Educational, Scientific, and Cultural Organization (UNESCO). (CRESALC has just been renamed IESALC, highlighting its status as an international institute.)

Research and policy can now also draw upon journals devoted to higher education, such as *Pensamiento Universitario* in Argentina, *Estudos e Debates* in Brazil, and *Reforma y Utopía* in Mexico. Country studies on Latin America appear in prominent international encyclopedias (Altbach 1991; Clark and Neave 1992), although the region remains only sporadically represented in most of the leading academic work produced in Western Europe and the United States on comparative higher education.

In this book, we provide a brief synthesis and analysis of the diverse experience of higher education in Latin American and link

---

[3] These overviews include Albornoz (1996), Balán and Trombetta (1996), Brunner (1990), Courard (1993), Drysdale (1987), García Guadilla (1996a), Kent (1996), Levy (1986), Maier and Weatherhead (1979), Navarro (1995), Schwartzman (1996a), Task Force (1994), Tedesco (1983), and Tyler et al. (1997).

[4] For an example of its continuing work on the region, see, for example, CPU (1990). For studies of higher education in Chile, see, for example, Krauskopf (1993).

that analysis to suggestions for policy reform. In particular, we address the principal myths that mischaracterize both the experience and the policies that could bring about positive reforms. We use the word "myth" not to mean a total falsehood, but rather a belief or even a collective dream based on something other than fact, often a belief in something exaggerated.

Although this book bases its arguments in the Latin American context, many of them are relevant elsewhere as well. We are keenly interested in any exploration of how this book's concepts, categories, assessments, and recommendations might be adapted to other developing and transition (including post-communist) regions. At the same time, there is a necessary geographical narrowing when it comes to the Caribbean. The book's generalizations fit the Dominican Republic and perhaps Haiti (adjusted for its poverty) much more than they fit Cuba or the English-speaking countries.[5]

Chapter 2 offers a brief assessment of the accomplishments and shortcomings of higher education in Latin America. Chapter 3 provides a historical sketch of how the traditional university evolved into a bewildering array of activities that are often poorly served by present policy. Chapter 4 presents a typology of the key functions of higher education—academic leadership, professional development, technological training and development, and general higher education. Chapter 5 applies the analysis and typology to three salient policy issues—subsidies, governance, and tools for quality control. Chapter 6 contrasts our main points to an internationally potent neoliberal agenda, highlighting differences as well as similarities.

---

[5] The English-speaking countries have a largely different tradition, which, in places such as the University of West Indies, escapes many debilitating syndromes that characterize higher education in Latin America.

CHAPTER 2

MIXED PERFORMANCE

Latin America has had a mixed performance in higher education. This apparently bland and unremarkable assessment stands out against the usual portrayals of higher education in the region. Defenders of the public university usually praise its role and powerful critics excoriate it. The laudatory view and the derogatory one both are based largely on myths.

The region has achieved poor average educational performance according to several measures: in comparison with most other regions, in relation to the level of social investment, and in comparison with prior educational performance. Yet, generalizations about poor performance subsume an extraordinary amount of variation and lead to a stereotype that provides a faulty basis for understanding reform. A review of the evidence shows a very complex picture. The predominantly negative assessment is accurate but incomplete. Leading scholars as well as officials tend to invoke a crisis rhetoric that is too generalized. Latin American educational systems have much that is right, including established tasks, widespread reforms in recent decades, and new changes underway.

Accomplishments

This section looks at higher education at work and its noneconomic contributions. It also discusses major reforms.

Higher Education at Work

One of the harshest and most general critiques claims that universities churn out hordes of graduates who are doomed to unemployment and underemployment. In reality, the job picture is more positive. Usually, wages reward and justify the students' efforts in higher education. Also, graduates have lower rates of unemployment.

In her study of Peru, Arregui (1994) finds what most studies in other countries find: individuals with some higher education earn more than those without, and individuals who graduate earn even more. In his study of Mexico, Vielle (in a discussion with the authors) reports that his empirical studies show that higher education does not over-subscribe or overproduce relative to the job market. Even those Mexicans with limited higher education get better jobs or earn more than others in the same jobs do. Follow-up studies at Mexico's Autonomous Metropolitan University find that these individuals obtain good jobs even when out of their field of study (Valenti et al. 1997).[1]

Overall, individual rates of return to higher education are good. This has been the case historically and remains so, even according to analyses by critics who decry rising unemployment and who blast publicly supported higher education (World Bank 1994, 1995). In fact, the critics turn positive individual rates of return into an argument for tuition, for charging those who directly benefit.[2]

Many of today's students are already in the workforce, providing further evidence of the link between higher education and employment. According to the persistent but mythical popular image, the typical student enters the university after secondary school and chooses a desired career at that point. But a survey of graduates from about 30 Brazilian institutions (sample size of over 20,000 respondents) shows a different profile (Castro and Spagnolo 1993). Students enter higher education at the average age of almost 30. Two-thirds of the students are employed in jobs that correspond to their degree programs. Most likely, students enroll in fields that fit the jobs they already hold and which they will likely retain after graduation (Castro and Spagnolo 1993).

---

[1] Empirical and economic studies give a much more positive picture of employment than conventional wisdom and stories. However, there is still a dearth of "tracer" studies, which explore what happens to graduates. Tracer studies are logical counterparts to help guide reforms that aim at making higher education institutions more efficient and more responsive to their societies—as they compete more for clientele and raise diverse revenue, including from alumni. See Muñoz Izquierdo and Lira (1990), Valenti et al. (1997), ANUIES (1998), Paul (1997), Magalhães Castro and Paul (1992), Castro and Spagnolo (1993), and OECD (1993a).

[2] The argument is bolstered to the extent that individual rates of return exceed social ones and to the extent they are high because students' education is publicly subsidized (rather than because the individual rises so high). Identification and denunciation of policies that produce such contrasts between individual and social returns emerge wherever higher education is free to the user (see, for example, Psacharopoulos 1988).

Box 2.1. The Taxi Driver Myth

The myth of the degree-holding taxi driver misleads the casual observer. As with the pencil vendor, the *taxista's* visibility provokes wildly exaggerated images. These are contradicted by the first hard data available. A Peruvian study estimates that only about 2 percent of those with some higher education drive a vehicle as either their primary or secondary job, and they earn probably twice the money made by Peruvians unable to attend higher education. In addition to *taxistas* doing short stints while waiting for a more desirable job, some people work as *taxistas* by choice and earn a decent income, escape harangues from office bosses, and even put their studies to profitable use by doing the accounting for groups of fellow workers (Arregui 1994).

Even at such a historic pillar as the University of Buenos Aires, two-thirds of the students are employed and half of the employed students work for more than 34 hours a week (Mollis 1995:19). Similarly, Latin America's typical master's degree student is not a full-time student and does not enter the program straight from an undergraduate program that was entered right after secondary school. Most of the National Autonomous University of Mexico's (UNAM's) master's degree students in education have at least 10 years of work experience, and most of the master's degree students in other fields have more than five; few claim they will spend 20 hours a week on academic studies (Esquivel forthcoming).

Those who believe that higher education overproduces by turning out too many graduates, including too many who are not well trained, should acknowledge that higher education continues to produce society's competent professionals (see box 2.1). Some studies claim that the data show a close fit between growth in higher education and growth in the real economy, notwithstanding charges to the contrary by business leaders (Lorey 1993). Chapter 5 looks in more detail at the social rates of return to higher education.

Noneconomic Contributions

Higher education has positively affected more than just the economy or the educational sector in a narrow sense. Critics often overlook this point, whereas universities invoke it too easily in order to steer attention away from economically and educationally measurable results. Different countries, policymakers, and social sectors seek different mixes of outcomes from higher education. The optimal results depend partly on values and political choices.

Universities in Latin America have promoted democracy or used the space available for critical thinking and expression within mostly authoritarian regimes. University-based intellectuals have enriched national thought, sometimes articulating alternatives to official policy and sometimes playing a major role in developing it. Universities in Latin America often have provided crucial channels of political modernization. For better or for worse, through their satisfaction of middle-class demands and promotion of national identity, universities have fostered political legitimacy and stability (Levy 1980).

Socially, universities have mobilized and delivered important services, such as health care. Places like the University of Buenos Aires have offered an open laical education in religious environments that could have been much more restrictive. Culturally, the public university often plays a vital role in producing and disseminating knowledge about the national patrimony as well as in building national identity. In both social and cultural respects, universities make various contributions not only through teaching, but also through research and extension.

Latin America leads the developing world in enrollments in higher education, with roughly one in five of the age cohort enrolled. It also ranks near the top in gender equality in enrollment. By 1980, women accounted for more than 40 percent of enrollments in most countries. In the late 1990s, given their majority in most large systems, women probably account for more than half of the regional total number of students in higher education, although typical differences emerge across fields of study. For example, until the 1960s in Brazil, very few women pursued university careers. By the late 1990s, women make up roughly 40 percent of the professors (Schwartzman 1996b:22–23).

Admittedly, this book pays less attention to such noneconomic factors than to the economic development matters that concern policymakers, including development banks. The dichotomy should not be overdrawn, however, because even the concerns of the banks have gone beyond purely economic issues. For example, in the 1990s the Inter-American Development Bank (IDB) increasingly has emphasized social development and the role and effective management of the state and its institutions. Moreover, we believe that much of what is socially, culturally, and politically desirable—and much of what is academically desirable—is consistent with sound economic policy. Indeed, higher education policy should have much to do with facilitating these varied aspects of development.

Reformed higher education policy should support technically sound and democratically progressive modernization.[3] Observers may legitimately differ on which reforms would best promote such modernization, but policies that run counter to sound economic criteria carry an extra burden of justification. Too many reform initiatives promoted from above marginalize noneconomic factors; at the same time, too much opposition to such reform, especially within public universities, marginalizes economic factors.

Reform Efforts

Critics often depict higher education as inadequate and woefully resistant to change. However, the record shows that the region has achieved significant reform over time, through both spontaneous processes and large-scale design.

The shifting fields of study illustrate the extent of spontaneous reform. According to the critics, higher education still produces mostly lawyers, doctors, and civil engineers. Yet, all three fields together account for less than one-third of enrollments (Levy 1986:268–71). New fields have sprung up within established universities and especially in new institutions, often led by a large and diverse private sector. The adaptation by field of study is one reason that higher education connects to the job market better than many think.[4] (See table 2.1 for enrollment in higher education by field of study.) And differences across fields illustrate the variation in the performance of universities. For example, although only one-third of those who enter Peruvian

---

[3] Those who have had the most to say about democracy in higher education are those opposed to increasingly dominant, neoliberal, international notions about the modernization of higher education. Of course, the earlier literature on student activism often had something to say about democratization. On the relationship between research centers and democratization in recent decades, see Puryear (1994) on Chile and Levy (1996a) on the region.

[4] A 1988 follow-up survey published in three national and three state newspapers in Mexico found that the greatest market demand existed for accountants, immediately followed by computer specialists. These are two of the areas of largest enrollment growth. It also turned out that law was overenrolled and did not offer the general mobility outside the profession that it once had.

Table 2.1. Enrollment in Higher Education by Field of Study, 1994

Country	Year	Education	Humanities	Social sciences, law, communications	Economics, business administration	Medical and health sciences	Natural sciences, math and statistics	Physical sciences, engineering, architecture and technology	Agronomy, veterinary studies and fishery	Unspecified	Total
Argentina	1994	12,214	84,281	163,600	148,737	131,212	39,959	124,765	25,444	10,263	740,475
Bolivia	1991	716	4,167	26,839	23,404	21,858	1,527	17,230	11,036	—	106,777
Brazil	1994	a	384,388	684,522	b	203,394	188,210	154,540	45,626	—	1,660,680
Chile	1994	26,037	39,437	58,235	68,001	17,052	8,073	82,254	27,995	—	327,084
Colombia	1993	91,814	21,422	66,010	162,387	47,927	7,374	147,920	16,369	—	561,223
Costa Rica	1994	14,483	4,189	24,820	a	5,292	3,966	7,635	1,962	15,726	78,073
Cuba	1994	72,040	—	16,686	7,681	36,660	5,923	28,886	8,352	—	176,228
Dom. Rep.	1988	a	12,335	45,732	b	10,347	—	28,422	—	—	96,836
Ecuador	1994	31,568	6,844	35,320	59,776	22,206	2,255	24,409	10,119	6,377	198,874
El Salvador	1994	7,535	11,080	23,198	22,918	15,133	2,650	18,822	1,199	—	102,535
Guatemala	1994	a	9,643	15,501	17,232	7,491	1,540	14,523	2,346	8,775c	77,051
Honduras	1994	1,761	4,313	12,226	13,734	6,563	1,383	11,130	2,219	437d	53,766
Mexico	1991	a	145,668	527,565	b	108,946	25,347	349,172	45,151	—	1,201,849
Nicaragua	1994	4,441	281	5,754	6,648	5,438	1,774	7,198	2,638	7,819	41,991
Panama	1993	2,447	b	11,739	12,944	2,709	2,520	10,927	788	—	44,074
Paraguay	1988e	154	2,994	8,948	5,010	2,731	3,208	5,083	806	1,497	30,431
Peru	1993	55,540	3,219	74,557	74,040	43,386	—	96,097 f	17,469	2,571	366,879
Uruguay	1994	256	1,158	4,533	2,537	1,056	1,850	—	424	—	11,814
Venezuela	1992	100,924	7,764	77,843	153,269	38,461	38,615	98,892	13,861	40,835	570,464
Total		421,930	743,183	1,883,628	778,318	727,862	336,174	1,227,905	233,804	94,300	6,447,104

— Not available.
a. Included in humanities.
b. Included in social sciences.
c. Regional centers.
d. Tourism.
e. Only public universities.
f. Includes natural sciences.
Source: García Guadilla (1996b:271).

universities graduate within six years, this indicator varies by field and institution between 1 and 97 percent (Arregui 1994).

Large reform by design has also sometimes worked. A key case concerns the alliance between domestic reformers and international agencies, which peaked in the 1960s and early 1970s. Analysts have regarded the alliance as disappointing because it failed to transform higher education into a vibrant enterprise approaching the institutions in industrial countries. Yet, by many reasonable criteria, the effort produced significant and worthwhile change. It contributed to greater social inclusiveness, inter-institutional differentiation, and functional differentiation, including organizational specialization in new technical, professional, and other fields. It greatly expanded the previously tiny instances of academic leadership at particular universities, research centers, and graduate programs, boosting the size of the true academic profession. Targeted institutions improved and surged ahead of untargeted ones.[5] Most of these achievements are obscured when assessments focus on average performance because most expansion occurred outside the bounds of these reforms. But the earlier reforms can light many paths for contemporary reform, including reinvigorated alliances between domestic and international partners in reform efforts.

Latin America has seen a surge in reform-by-design efforts in recent years (Courard 1993; Task Force 1994; Kent 1996). Accreditation, for example, has grown from almost zero into an influential movement. Like other highlights of the contemporary public policy reform agenda, reform of higher education proceeds concretely in some places and at least commands increased attention in others. There are parallels in a range of academic, governance, and financial reforms.

Successful reform lifts much performance above the negative stereotype. At the national level, differences across countries in the overall level of development account for different levels of performance, but so does variation in reform efforts across countries. Countries that participated amply in reform by design in the 1960s and 1970s have shown payoffs, for example, in construction of viable new public universities, departments, and graduate education. Over the last decade, Chile has implemented a relatively successful market-oriented reform of its national higher education system (Brunner,

---

[5] Even where projects did not produce as anticipated, they often made noteworthy changes, for example, in departments in institutions or in research and graduate programs outside universities.

Courard, and Cox 1992). Although we do not consider it a panacea for other countries to copy exactly, the country's reform efforts include several pathbreaking features. Institutional autonomy has played a role in innovative student and financial markets. State subsidization has yielded substantially to mixed private and public funding, while performance-based state funding has increased (Lemaitre 1990; Lemaitre and Lavados 1986). Costly university enrollments have been held in check while other institutions have responded to the demand for post-secondary education, and evaluation systems have been created (Brunner 1992; Persico 1992).

Some observers might dismiss the Chilean case because it is too exceptional. Indeed, the literature repeatedly refers to Chile's higher education system in support of internationally promoted reform efforts. It is important to note other breakthroughs that few people thought were possible several years ago (Wolff and Albrecht 1992). For example, Argentina's new national legislation allows public institutions to charge tuition and establish their own admissions policies. Venezuela and most other countries have undertaken less public policy reform, but they have at least inaugurated important debate (on Venezuela, see Lovera 1994). Mexico epitomizes an evolving discussion about reform efforts. Some analysts say that the initiatives dwarf real change. Others argue that change has been too great, spurred by Mexico's admission to the Organization for Economic Cooperation and Development (OECD). It is clear that the government has made higher education fit the international neoliberal reform agenda (Levy 1998a). While there is merit in some of the critiques, we agree with national experts who perceive noteworthy change (see box 2.2).

At the sector level, where public higher education has changed too little or too slowly to meet student or job market demand, private institutions have often jumped into the void (Levy 1986).[6] Many private institutions have emerged to absorb student demand that is not met by the public sector, despite that sector's major and often maligned expansion. Table 2.2 shows the number of private and public institutions of higher education.

---

[6] Empirical studies of private higher education finally appeared in some countries in the 1990s. The most extensive is the NUPES project (see Sampaio 1998). Several studies have included the private sector and private-public comparisons (for example, Kent 1996, 1997). Among short works of regional scope, see Balán and Fanelli (1997) and Levy (1993). For works on private higher education beyond Latin America, see Geiger (1986), Altbach (1999), and Levy (1992).

Box 2.2. Mexican Public Universities Introduce Reforms

Mexico's new national policies have reportedly had a notable impact in several previously unexceptional state universities and even in some that bordered on the stereotypically inefficient and politicized (Ornelas 1996; Kent 1998). The Autonomous University of Puebla has cut its total enrollment by one-third, partly by tightening access through standardized testing, curtailing the endless retaking of course examinations, and cutting loose many quasi-students. It has moved toward a credit system and a common group of general introductory courses, revamped the curriculum, improved efficiency in producing graduates, and advanced the whole process by abolishing universal voting by the university community for administrative authorities.

Most public universities now charge a meaningful, if modest, tuition and many actively seek other income from nongovernmental sources. The universities increasingly use a nonprofit national evaluation center to help screen student applications.

In most nations, private higher education started with Catholic universities, moved on to elite secular universities, and then increasingly involved demand-absorbing institutions. The majority of the private institutions, especially the newer ones, exhibit profound weaknesses that should preoccupy the citizenry and policymakers; however, others are academically serious and innovative. Many private institutions, while far from the classical conception of a university, are specialized institutions finding their niche within their nation's rapidly diversifying job market—the sort of niche increasingly found by private institutions in Asia, Africa, and the transition economies in Eastern and Central Europe (Levy 1999b). Fields such as business, management, administration, tourism, marketing, and accounting show a higher education response to international political-economic change. Importantly, where the region's private (or public) institutions do reasonably well in any of the four functions (academic leadership, professional development, technological training and development, and general higher education), a failure to conform to vaunted notions of what a "real university" should be is not evidence of unworthiness.

Comparing public and private institutions of higher education reveals more overlap between the sectors than superior performance in

Table 2.2. The Number of Public and Private Higher Education Institutions, 1994

Country	Year	Universities			Other institutions			Total		
		Public	Private	Total	Public	Private	Total	Public	Private	Total
Argentina	1994	37	42	79	956	718[a]	1,674	993	760	1,753
Bolivia	1995	11	24	35	44	2	46	55	26	81
Brazil	1994	68	59	127	150	574	724	218	633	851
Chile	1995	25[b]	45	70	–	200	200	25	245[c]	270
Colombia	1994	51	96	147	28	83	111	79	179	258
Costa Rica	1994	4	20	24	68	207[d]	275	72	227	299
Cuba	1994	7	–	7	28	–	28	35	–	35
Dom. Rep.	1995	1	24	25	6	4	10	7	28	35
Ecuador	1995	15	8	23[e]	73	78	151	88	86	174
El Salvador	1995	2	44	46	17	10	27	19	54	73
Guatemala	1994	1	5	6	1	2	3	2	7	9
Honduras	1995	2	4	6	2	3	5	4	7	11
Mexico	1995	39	49	88	383	199	582	422	248	670
Nicaragua	1994	4	7	11	–	3	3	4	10[f]	14
Panama	1994	3	13	16	1	4	5	4	17	21
Paraguay	1994	3	12	15	39	18	57	42	30	72
Peru	1993	28	25	53	347	277	624	375	302	677
Uruguay	1995	1	1	2	10	9	19	11	10	21[g]
Venezuela	1994	17	15	32	43	39	82	60	54	114
Total		319	493	812	2,196	2,430	4,626	2,515	2,923	5,438

– Not available.
a. 10 undetermined institutions added.
b. 16 public universities and 9 private universities with state aid.
c. Institutions that do not get direct state aid.
d. Includes 176 institutions not recognized by the Ministry of Education.
e. Some universities are functional but are not legalized and therefore are not in the national university council.
f. Includes some that receive state aid.
g. The Instituto de Formación Docente, which trains teachers for the primary and pre-primary level, has 25 campuses.
Source: García Guadilla (1996b:264).

one. For example, Brazil has roughly one-third of the region's private enrollments (see table 2.3). In contrast to public institutions elsewhere in the region, public universities in Brazil have competitive entrance examinations and very high annual student expenses (nearly $10,000 in some places). INEP (1997) and Sampaio (1998) describe the first comprehensive database on higher education in Brazil. The database comes from a survey of students one semester before graduation in civil engineering, business administration, and law. It contains the number of students with top grades (A grades) and the distribution of grades. In the sample, 13 percent of the institutions are private. Public universities

Table 2.3.   Enrollment in Public and Private Higher Education Institutions, 1994
(thousands)

Country	Public			Private			Total		
	Universities	Other institutions	Total	Universities	Other institutions	Total	Universities	Other institutions	Total
Argentina	618.4	221.8	840.2	124.7	89.2	213.9	743.1	311.0	1,054.1
Bolivia	124.5	16.5	141.0	12.3	0.7	13.0	136.9	17.2	154.0
Brazil	571.6	118.8	690.4	463.1	507.5	970.6	1,034.7	626.3	1,661.0
Chile	151.6	—	151.6	60.0	115.5	175.5	211.6	115.5	327.1
Colombia[a]	135.5	65.7	201.2	232.9	127.1	360.0	386.4	192.8	561.2
Costa Rica	60.7	2.9	63.6	17.5	2.5	20.0	78.2	5.4	83.6
Cuba	36.8	139.5	176.2	—	—	—	36.8	139.5	176.2
Dominican Republic	32.4	—	32.4	77.8	2.5	80.4	110.3	2.5	112.8
Ecuador	154.5[b]	9.0	163.5	44.4	5.1	49.5	198.9	14.1	213.0
El Salvador	30.5	2.9	33.4	72.5	2.1	74.7	103.0	5.0	108.1
Guatemala	80.2	—	80.2	30.8	1.6	32.4	111.0	1.6	112.6
Honduras	46.7	0.3	47.1	6.0	0.7	6.7	52.7	1.1	53.8
Mexico[c]	751.3	223.8	975.1	145.5	183.5	329.0	896.8	407.3	1,304.1
Nicaragua[d]	27.6	—	27.6	12.8	1.5	14.4	40.4	1.6	42.0
Panama[e]	63.2	0.5	63.7	5.6	0.3	5.9	68.7	0.8	69.5
Paraguay	20.1	8.0	28.1	21.7	3.0	24.7	41.8	11.0	52.9
Peru	237.2	174.9	412.1	129.7	101.4	231.1	366.9	276.3	643.2
Uruguay	62.0	8.3	70.3	2.0	2.5	4.5	64.0	10.8	74.8
Venezuela	325.7	61.5	387.2	80.7	133.2	213.9	406.4	194.7	601.1
Total	3,530.7	1,054.4	4,585.0	1,540.1	1,280.1	2,820.2	5,070.7	2,334.5	7,405.3

a. 1993.
b. Does not include data from the Universidad Politécnica Salesiana and the Universidad de San Francisco de Quito.
c. Institutions affiliated with the National Association of Universities and Institutes of Higher Education (ANUIES).
d. In the private sector, this includes universities and other institutions that are private but receive 6 percent of their funds as state aid. No information was obtained from two institutions.
e. For universities, the data are from three universities that represent the majority of the enrollments. For other institutions, the data are estimated.
Source: García Guadilla (1996b:270).

have twice as many students with top grades compared with private universities. The overall distribution of grades shows no clear superiority of public over private universities. Almost as many fields of study show a higher average grade level in private universities as show a higher average grade level in public universities. Public universities dominate in the number of students with the lowest grade level. For those who believe in the value or even the near inevitability of robust higher education expansion, growth of private institutions has value if their academic quality overlaps that of public institutions.

The value of expansion of private higher education increases for those who believe in much of what powerful international higher education calls for: inter-institutional differentiation, private funding, a more rigorous and intelligent regulatory role for the state, improved scores in standard efficiency measures, and limited political conflict, among other factors (Carlson 1992; World Bank 1994; Levy 1998b). In some countries, private institutions have recently contributed greatly to the idea of inter-institutional competition. Even for observers who hold mixed or negative views of these ideas, the implementation of them certainly undermines critiques of Latin American higher education as unchanging.

Furthermore, certain private institutions have engaged in voluntary agreements or consortiums with one another or with public institutions, thereby building useful coordination into the system without building in excessive central control. Many good private institutions make a reasonable claim that they perform a useful public service, with private funds and management.[7]

Private higher education accounts for nearly 40 percent of the enrollments in the region and nearly 60 percent in Brazil (see table 2.3). The Catholic and elite secular universities usually boast an academic, economic, and political importance (influence, mobility to high office, etc.) that transcends their share of undergraduate enrollments. However, the public sector has proportionally greater weight at the graduate level, especially the doctoral level (see table 2.4). Nations that lacked elite secular institutions have created them in the 1980s and 1990s (for example, Argentina and Chile). Thus, a serious assess-

---

[7] In this book, the term private is a legal designation that is usually, but not always, indicative of aspects of finance and management, but does not presume either lesser or greater worth for society.

Table 2.4. Enrollment in Graduate Higher Education, 1994

Country	Year	Doctoral programs			Master's program			Specialization programs			All graduate programs	
		Public	Private	Total	Public	Private	Total	Public	Private	Total	Public	Total
Argentina[a]	1994	1,804	251	2,055	2,144	1,516	3,660	3,926	449	4,375	7,874	10,090
Bolivia	1994	—	—	—	717	589	1,306	509	98	607	1,226	1,913
Brazil	1994	14,373	1,299	15,672	33,692	5,257	38,949	—	—	—	48,065	54,621
Chile	1994	71	5	76	4,332	166	4,498[b]	2,629	207	2,836	6,961	7,334
Colombia	1993	—	—	—	2,900	3,338	6,238	5,245	12,453	17,698	8,216	24,012
Costa Rica	1994	—	—	—	1,022	—	1,022	196	—	196	1,218	1,218
Cuba	1994	267	—	267	2,142	—	2,142	8,209	—	8,209	10,618	10,618
El Salvador	1995	—	—	—	180	280	460	—	—	—	180	450
Guatemala	1995	—	—	—	451	—	451	596	—	596	1,047	1,047
Honduras	1994	—	—	—	115	36	151	131	—	131	246	282
Mexico	1993	1,901	250	2,151	22,207	8,983	31,190	14,056	3,384	17,440	38,164	50,781
Nicaragua	1994	—	—	—	181	—	181	526	—	526	707	707
Panama	1994	—	—	—	244	86	330	741	—	741	985	1,071
Paraguay	1995	—	—	—	210	194	404	110	40	150	320	554
Peru	1993	167	755	922	2,057	3,535	5,592	481	230	711	2,705	7,255
Uruguay[c]	1994	122	—	122	196	—	196	—	—	—	318	318
Venezuela	1995	829	—	829	4,740	458	5,198	5,918	1,197	7,115	11,487	13,141
Total		19,534	2,560	22,094	77,530	24,438	101,968	43,273	18,058	61,331	140,337	185,393

— Not available.
a. Partial data.
b. Includes doctoral programs.
c. Includes only students in basic sciences at the Universidad de la República.
Note: There are no data available for the Dominican Republic and Ecuador.
Source: García Guadilla (1996b:276).

ment of Latin American higher education must appreciate both the public and private sectors.

At the same time, public higher education in some countries has achieved important reforms. Where established universities were slow to change, new ones were sometimes created as alternatives (for example, Venezuela's Simón Bolívar, Brazil's Campinas, and Colombia's Valle). Argentina provides interesting examples from both the 1970s and more recently (Taquini 1972; García de Fanelli 1997; Mignone 1992). Other public universities, such as Peru's Cayetano Heredia in medicine and related science, have become more specialized by task. The specialized universities, in particular, do not replicate the national universities' objective of covering all or nearly all academic fields. Public technological institutes have proliferated—while academic study of them lags shamefully—and usually differ from universities in function as well as governance. A more detailed analysis would show that even the largest public universities, those with daunting problems overall, have managed to achieve significant reforms in some of their programs and activities.[8]

Stereotypes about an essentially unchanging higher education do not hold up; they are myths. A variety of forces have driven a variety of reforms, a point that is further illustrated by Latin America's growing islands of research.

Islands of Research

Judged by its overall output and typical university programs, Latin America's performance in research falls far short of both expectations and claims. However, the region has made significant advances. It produces much more high-quality research today than it did decades ago. National and other public higher education institutions usually account for a major share of research in the region; some conventional indicators credit them with roughly 80 percent of the research and, likewise, a major share of the national science and technology effort.

---

[8] The introduction of science programs is a good example, especially because exact and natural sciences often avoid some problems plaguing other fields and maintain more serious academic policies. At the University of Buenos Aires, for example, hard science is joined by medicine, but even the philosophy program earns praise.

The research gains are hardly limited to a few institutions. Indeed, the gains provide further testimony of the benefits of reform through institutional diversification. Some universities have protected research within a few outstanding programs. Others have established serious research centers outside their troubled or inefficient programs; for example, the science institutes of Mexico's National University (Fortes and Lomnitz 1991). In addition, several universities and institutes combine teaching and research in a specialized field, such as agriculture or medicine. Many fine public research centers operate with links to ministries (Alvarez and Gómez 1994; Adler 1987; Brunner 1991). Like public universities, the public research centers receive government money, but they often surpass the public universities in management flexibility, incentive structures, and relationships with external actors (Levy 1996a). Venezuela's Institute for Scientific Research (IVIC) is a prime example (Vessuri 1997).

Latin America has added a welcome proliferation of private research centers, for example, Argentina's Center for Social Research (CICSO), Brazil's São Paulo Institute of Political, Social, and Economic Studies (IDESP), Chile's Corporation of Economic Research for Latin America (CIEPLAN), Guatemala's Association for Research and Social Studies (ASIES), the Paraguayan Center of Sociological Studies (CPES), Peru's Group of Development Analysis (GRADE), Venezuela's Institute of Advanced Administrative Studies (IESA), and the Latin American Faculty of Social Science (FLACSO) in Ecuador. Often these centers arose not from a national plan, but actually in opposition to mainstream public policy (Brunner and Barrios 1987). Along with many public and university research centers and private universities, but often more so, the private research centers defy stereotypes about Latin American higher education. They are quicker to evolve, to adapt to shifting environments, and to innovate in ways beyond the abilities of the public universities. Private research centers often operate in competitive markets, earn their own money, and govern themselves. They are among the most international educational organizations in terms of the flow of ideas and resources. They are important in social and policy research, and sometimes in related graduate training, although rarely in basic science and technology. Private research centers serve democratic governments, businesses, and a surging group of grassroots and advocacy nongovernmental organizations. Of course, they also suffer from problems and serious shortcomings (Levy 1996a; Calderón and Provoste 1990).

Indeed, we do not want to glorify any of the alternative institutional and functional arrangements. Each has limitations; none is a full substitute for an academically first-rate university. But the alternative institutions show the oversimplifications in the common critiques of higher education in the region. Differentiation in the region is enormous and highlights the need for assessments and policies that are similarly differentiated.

Finally, some research is propitiously blended with graduate education, although most growth in the region's graduate enrollments must be placed more on the negative side of the ledger—limited in research and academic standing (Albornoz 1996). Estimable pockets of quality exist in Mexico and especially Brazil and, to a lesser extent, Argentina (García de Fanelli 1996), Chile (Gazmuri 1992; Letelier 1992), and other countries (Tedesco 1992; Lucio 1997). Some master's programs without strong research programs insert themselves into the job market or otherwise support social development.

As we turn now to concentrate on troubling realities, we should not lose sight of the positive features highlighted to this point. Higher education has performed better than often depicted regarding the world of work. It has contributed to vital noneconomic aspects of development. And it has reformed in a variety of ways, often creating estimable pockets of success alongside or even within more problematic structures.

Shortcomings

Despite its positive features, higher education in the region suffers from severe shortcomings. Identification of the shortcomings provides a vital step toward tackling and diminishing them.

Higher education in Latin America is in widespread disrepair, plagued by crises of legitimacy, ill-defined labor markets for graduates, and damaging social and political confrontations. In turn, poor performance breeds ill will toward higher education and uncooperative defensiveness from many advocates for higher education. This book endeavors to juxtapose achievements and shortcomings to provide a balanced picture. However, leading scholars have diagnosed the higher education systems in their countries and in the region and found them woeful in performance. See, for example, Balán and Trombetta (1996),

Brunner (1993), Brunner et al. (1995), Contreras (1996), Neave and van Vught (1994), and Schwartzman (1998).

Some of the shortcomings have resulted from ill-conceived practices in higher education. Others have resulted primarily from inadequate response to problems or changes emanating elsewhere. Of course, honest and informed observers who agree substantially on identification of the shortcomings do not always agree on their source. Nonetheless, we focus on what higher education itself and those concerned with it can do to improve the situation. Thus, subsequent sections of the book may appear unfair in not dwelling more on problems imposed upon higher education, just as they may appear unfair in devoting more time to shortcomings and policy changes than to elaborating on the accomplishments to date.

Average Educational Performance

Most institutions turn in an educational performance below reasonable expectations. Serious debate now usually accepts that and focuses largely on how low is low or on what causes the disappointing performance and what to do about it.

Much of the explanation for higher education's difficulties lies with the huge, accelerated expansion launched in mid-century. The expansion weakened established institutions and usually did not create strong new institutions. This was a worldwide problem (Trow 1974; OECD 1993b); however, it had an extreme manifestation in Latin America. Defenders of the expansion who decry the term "massification" because enrollment rates still only reach a minority and remain lower than in industrial countries do not face this reality (Borón 1995). By 1981, the percentage of Peru's population with some higher education approximated the percentage in England and was twice as large as the percentage in Italy; by 1993, the figure doubled in Peru (Arregui 1994). In Mexico, the problems caused by access for underprepared students have been aggravated by the practice of preferential admission from the national university's preparatory level into higher education programs. Countries like the Dominican Republic also face major challenges in higher education from rapid growth in secondary education (Fernández 1980).

The acceleration of enrollments in higher education in Latin America took place within the context of economic underdevelopment and instability, technological backwardness, and dependence. In addition, higher education suffered from political repression and turmoil, and cultural indifference to science and research. Rising enrollments meant that expenditures kept rising. In some cases, such as Venezuela and Colombia in the 1980s, expenditures rose in absolute terms while they fell in per student terms. Higher education grew much faster than the base of adequately prepared teachers and administrators, including secondary school graduates and professors. Latin America's higher education enrollment rates lagged behind those in Europe by only about a decade, while other measures of higher, secondary, and basic education, as well as overall socioeconomic development, lagged by much more (Levy 1986:40–41). The link between Latin America's substantial enrollment growth and its problems with average performance does not necessarily argue against large or growing higher education systems. Evaluators must recognize that responsible growth would have required degrees of preparation and nourishment that the region could not or would not provide.

Hence, beyond the mediocrity of average educational results per se, what is troubling is the combination of a major outlay of public resources and comparatively paltry results for both students and society. Many of the difficulties stem from factors outside higher education itself; however, higher education institutions and other institutions, including governments, need to undertake fundamental reform.

Efficiency and Qualitative Indicators

Standard measures of efficiency are too low to brush aside even though they are inexact (Wolff and Albrecht 1992; World Bank 1994). Often the data refer principally to public universities, the institutions that still account for the bulk of enrollments and expenditures.

Reports on internal efficiency find a lack of institutional planning, management, and monitoring and accountability (Winkler 1990). The number of students per professor is low, as is the number of students per administrator. Too many of the entrants never graduate or spend far longer in school than the estimated duration of the program. Fixed budgets are too high when compared with flexible or performance-based expenditures. The portion of the budget allocated to personnel costs is disproportionately high, compared with investment in infrastructure. Most indicators show a magnitude that should place a heavy burden of proof on those who would like to dismiss them.

At the same time, most private universities are academically weak. Even the stronger private universities and freestanding centers tend to be rather small, narrow in scope, and marginal to basic research and advanced education (particularly in scientific and other costly fields). Their competency often lacks academic meaning. While certain forms of privatization have greatly improved higher education's typically low performance as well as its efficiency, and should be expanded, other forms are dubious. Privatization is far from an effective cure-all, and there are worthy and unworthy private institutions as well as worthy and unworthy public ones.

Furthermore, although the numbers of full-time professors, publications, and graduate programs may be initially impressive, they do not reflect the academic development supposedly associated with the nomenclature. Thus, only a minority of "full-time" professors dedicate at least 40 hours a week to teaching and serious research (see table 2.5). The quality of performance usually falls well short of what most observers associate with academic professionalism.

Thus, qualitative indicators buttress the negative profile on efficiency. Although they are not unique to the region, the following maladies are often seen in Latin American higher education: rote learning, outdated curricula, lack of pedagogical materials, and laxity in access to and passage through the system. Many students and professors lack the proper preparation to learn and teach. Many institutions lack basic materials.

Internal conflict is natural within public institutions, notably those that value participation and debate. However, many universities have not met the difficult challenge of reconciling conflict with the need for sound academic and economic policy. Where detrimental conflict and other political factors penetrate too far into academic affairs, they sustain policies that benefit certain individuals and groups in the short run, but that suppress the development of teaching and research. Those concerned about the fate of higher education in Latin America must face this situation, even if they properly resist the stereotype of omnipresent hyper-politicization. In addition, as in Argentina and Chile, the most severe damage to academic freedom and performance has sometimes resulted from military repression. In Central America, Colombia, and Peru, it has resulted from other violent national politics or a combination of that and repressive dictatorship (Brunner and Barrios 1987; Levy 1981; Puryear 1982).

Table 2.5. The Number of Professors, by Time Commitment, 1994

Country	Year	Public				Private			
		Full time	Half time	By course	Total	Full time	Half time	By course	Total
Argentina[a]	1992	11,550	21,498	68,203	101,251	—	—	—	—
Brazil	1994	52,863	22,422	—	75,285	9,118	57,079	—	66,197
Chile[b]	1994	7,537	2,175	6,802	16,514	—	—	—	—
Colombia	1993	9,805	2,312	8,382	20,499	4,376	2,085	29,263	35,724
Costa Rica	1994	1,524	528	1,229	3,281	894	310	721	1,925
Cuba	1994	23,339	—	782	24,121	—	—	—	—
El Salvador	1994	1,558	445	222	2,225	382	611	2,827	3,820
Honduras	1994	2,151	258	793	3,202	231	184	238	653
Mexico	1994	40,603	12,765	92,001	145,369	4,123	2,276	24,199	30,598
Nicaragua	1994	1,329	322	490	2,141	290	52	201	543
Panama	1994	1,459	—	2,337	3,796	44	4	321	369
Peru	1995	6,854	4,629	6,702	18,185	213	1,793	6,688	8,694
Uruguay[c]	1995	976	3,072	3,057	7,105	—	—	—	—
Venezuela	1995	13,004	1,823	3,976	18,803	—	—	—	—
Total		174,552	72,249	194,976	441,777	19,671	64,394	64,458	148,523

a. Only universities.

b. Only for the 25 universities with direct state aid.

c. Includes only the Universidad de la República.

Note: There are no data available for Bolivia, the Dominican Republic, Ecuador, Guatemala, and Paraguay.

Source: García Guadilla (1996b:279).

New technologies and organizational innovations affect the transmission and generation of knowledge throughout the world. The traditional model, in which the classroom centers on a lecturer, has become one option among many. Computers, videos, television, and the Internet create an array of new alternatives, including modular learning strategies. The geographical boundaries of teaching and the physical location of resources are less restrictive. Modern technology has altered the fundamental logic and economics of knowledge transmission. However, Latin American higher education has remained distant from these trends, with the exception of the pioneering efforts of some institutions. The majority of the institutions have foregone many of the benefits of technological progress; they risk being bypassed by more aggressive institutions, such as those providing distance education through the Internet.

The shortcomings of higher education often translate into a troubling loss of legitimacy and prestige. Employers, funders, scholars in the field of education, and others laboring within higher education perceive a dismal and worsening situation. Many critics pour abuse on the public universities, blaming them for ills that go well beyond their responsibility or reasonable ability to solve alone. In this book, we attempt to focus more on improvement rather than blame.

Compounding all the identified weaknesses, and notwithstanding the reforms noted above, is the fact that these weaknesses too rarely generate the kind of political or administrative reaction that would lead to their correction. Higher education in Latin America suffers from a lack of incentives for improvement. Each of the main forces that propel sounder higher education elsewhere has been weak in Latin America. Examples include accountability to consumers or funders, helpful state controls, and a strong academic ethos. To employ Clark's (1983) already classic formulation, we observe that the market, the state, and the academic oligarchy have all failed to play an adequate role in the region.

A vital concern for public policy and, therefore, for this book, is the disconnection between performance and the reward structure. There are too few rewards for good performance and too few sanctions for incompetence or irresponsibility. Impunity and perpetuation of the status quo translate into major shortcomings in performance.

CHAPTER 3

DIFFERENTIATED AND COMPLEX SYSTEMS

In Latin America's differentiated and complex systems of higher education, some institutions perform better than others do and some do basically different things. Failure to recognize important differences contributes to the myths that produce flawed diagnoses and improper starting points for reforming policy.

The term "university," used as a loose synonym for higher education, obscures the differences among institutions of higher education. Although some analysts refer to differentiation, few include it as an integral part of their analyses and policy recommendations. Indeed, some institutions that are not called universities do a large share of what is traditionally conceived of as university work. At the same time, and much more commonly, some institutions that are called universities do little such work.

Here we look at the evolution of new roles in higher education and the costs of mislabeling institutions.

Evolution of New Roles

Much of the confusion in terminology stems from the diffusion and complexity that has emerged over time. In the late Middle Ages, European nation-states created universities for the study of subjects such as theology, philosophy, and law. Those generally prestigious institutions catered to the elite. Subsequently, professional schools emerged in engineering, medicine, architecture, fine arts, and other areas of study. Some professional schools stood alone, others were loosely affiliated into what was called the Napoleonic university. With some alterations, this became the Continental model (Clark 1977, 1983). It was exported to Europe's colonies and ex-colonies, but rarely in pure form (Steger 1979; Lanning 1971). It was also imported, emulated, and modified by the elite within the colonies, who sought a link between the establishment of universities and national development (Mollis 1990; Serrano 1993).

The Continental model has the following key features: a large state that grants authority to chaired professors, professional programs with considerable power, and weak central administration of the university. The power of the professors grew where the German or Humboltean influence emerged, starting late in the nineteenth century. This influence added the focus on science, research, and the practical application of knowledge (for example, medicine, pharmacy, and mining). The emphasis on practical applications resurfaced when links with the U.S. land grant colleges were established. More broadly, the U.S. university model became the new beacon in the postwar period. This model was based on centralized institutions, with departments (rather than separate programs), campuses, full-time teachers and students, and a limited role for government, especially national government.[1]

Each of these foreign models inspired Latin America at different times, but not with equal impact. The Napoleonic and Continental forms had the biggest formative impact, especially given the Spanish and Portuguese colonial heritage and the strong French influence when the region achieved independence. An exception, Brazil relied on free-standing professional schools until the 1930s.

Despite noteworthy inroads, the impact of German and U.S. ideals has been so sporadic as to render the university nomenclature usually an empty shell. There are more universities by law or loose usage than by conventional tasks and performance. Some universities are just bad institutions; some are glorified high schools. Others are worthy according to functions not connected to or not requiring university status (for example, fine teaching for professional, technological, or general education). Most institutions do not have graduate and research programs (see table 3.1). Furthermore, graduate studies usually consist of specialized programs that have less to do with internationally recognizable academic excellence than with professional preparation, sometimes reflecting the inadequacy of that preparation at the undergraduate level. Today, most institutions that are called universities are only weakly linked with excellence.

A few universities have achieved overall academic distinction; however, some of the region's most outstanding academic institutions are not universities. Like the French *Grandes Ecoles*, they often distin-

---

[1] For an overview and analysis of these and other higher education models, see Clark (1995).

Table 3.1. The Number of Higher Education Institutions with and without Graduate and Research Programs, 1990s

Country	Institutions with graduate and research programs	Institutions with only under-graduate programs	Total
Argentina	10	69	79[a]
Bolivia	11	24	35[a]
Brazil	91	760	851
Chile	33[b]	62	95
Colombia	69	180	249
Costa Rica	4	20	24[a]
Cuba	35	—	35
Dominican Republic	25	—	25[a]
Ecuador	10	19	29
El Salvador	8	38	46[a]
Guatemala	5	1	6[a]
Honduras	2	9	11
Mexico	—	—	—
Nicaragua	4	10	14
Panama	13	1	14[a]
Paraguay	2	13	15[a]
Peru	26	27	53[a]
Uruguay	2	19	21
Venezuela	26	88	114
Total	376	1,340	1,716

— Not available.
a. Includes only universities.
b. Some private institutions offer graduate degrees with foreign institutions.
Source: García Guadilla (1996b).

guish themselves more through training than research. Brazil's Ouro Preto School of Mines provides a superb approximation of some French schools in engineering. Unfortunately, by the time it became a university, the quality of the school had dropped precipitously.

Among the leaders in research and areas of related service, public and private research centers exist within or outside universities, sometimes in direct response to shortcomings in the university's mainstream (Levy 1996a). Academic leadership indicators include the num-

Box 3.1. When Rules and Functions Collide

- A creative physicist published the two decisive books laying the groundwork for the creation of the electric microphone. Had he patented the device, he and his university would have earned millions of dollars. But existing rules did not provide for funding of applied science, much less for patenting fees.
- Many universities have more teachers on full-time contracts than teachers with even a master's education. Since the full-time contract is meant to ensure that teachers do research, it essentially asks them to undertake an activity for which they lack preparation.
- Rules may require five years or more to change curriculum in a technical college, but in areas such as electronics and computers, curricula often become obsolete in a much shorter period.
- Committees meet for years to detail the program curricula and syllabi, engaging in discussions of theory and doctrine in the discipline, and fighting to decide on the worthwhile developments in the area. At the same time, few graduates of many of the programs may work in occupations corresponding directly to their diplomas.
- A premier mining engineering school was celebrated for its high standards and the technological leadership of the students it produced for well over half a century. But it was pushed to become a university, by adding more students and different programs. It has become a mediocre middle-sized university.

ber of advanced degrees earned by students, the number of publications in top journals, and useful consultant appointments that serve public or private sponsors. Few Latin American universities approximate the ideal typical university characteristics as well as Mexico's El Colegio de Mexico and Center of Research and Advanced Studies (CINVESTAV) or Brazil's Escola Paulista de Medicina or Rio de Janeiro University Research Institute (IUPERJ) or ITA.

The separation of research from teaching goes against a major tenet of the U.S. or German research university ideal. Most of Latin America's freestanding research centers do not have formal graduate programs, and university research centers usually undertake only limited teaching. Universities that perform academic leadership functions do so only within certain units. The units that do the best research and advanced academic teaching are almost always part of disjointed conglomerates that, as a whole, produce more bad, useless, or marginal than good research. Thus, national universities in many countries (for example, Colombia, Guatemala, and Venezuela) deserve accolades for their enclaves of academic leadership; however, these universities in general produce mediocre academic work and professional development of variable quality.

Universities that achieve academic homogeneity at high levels are mostly small, and most of these are very limited in basic research and graduate education. Brazil's (public) State University of Campinas (UNICAMP) may come about as close as any university of substantial size to fitting the conventional image of a university. Leading Catholic universities are much closer than most Latin American institutions to research universities, but they tend to focus on professional and quasi-professional functions rather than academic leadership functions.[2]

In recent decades, institutions of higher education have introduced technical fields of study that were not envisioned in most of the foreign models just identified.[3] Often, lower-level technical training schools as well as normal schools taught courses in these fields, which were pushed up to the post-secondary level. In addition, some new occupations, including some that people once learned on the job, now require more complex, formal training. The courses vary in duration (for example, Brazil's Centros Federais de Tecnologia is a four-year course of study). Some programs reside within institutions that offer mostly four- to six-year courses; others have appeared in separate, new institutions. Some of the new institutions are called universities, for example, in Costa Rica, but even where they do not don the university nomenclature, they often pursue the benefits of official political parity and parallel treatment. Policymakers show scarce ability to understand and design policies that are adequate to this additional differentiation across and within higher education institutions.

---

[2] Except for a handful of institutions like those in the Ivy League, few universities anywhere achieve a nearly uniform high academic level; the point here is that Latin America is far from even that approximation.

[3] In industrial countries, concern for the practical stimulated the growth of technical or technological higher education. In Latin America, the creation of formal, separate sectors mimicked those in Europe; where technological functions drifted into a variety of institutions, there was a more U.S. flavor.

In short, diffusion has contributed to confusion about roles and responsibilities. Latin Americans have come to use the term university as a catch-all that has connotations and pretenses that rarely conform to the diverse forms and functions that now characterize higher education in the region. Overall, there is a huge gap between the myth and reality of the university.

Costs of Mislabeling

The mislabeling of institutions contributes to policies that are inappropriate for the real functions performed and also to imbalances among the functions.[4] Mislabeling gives rise to four main problems. First, with too many policies of the one-size-fits-all type, different institutions, units, and individuals receive the same treatment. Policies of standardization (*homologación* or *isonomia* in Brazil) treat all alike and reinforce the tendency of institutions to aspire or claim to be what they are not. In modified form, when technical sectors are created and recognized alongside university sectors, two sizes are supposed to fit all. Yet, the same rules do not make sense for different activities or for similar activities at different levels of performance.

The inappropriateness of similar treatment for different institutions is highlighted in cases where technical institutions were created precisely because they differ from existing universities. Similar treatment leads to ill-defined status for the new courses and to ill-defined job markets for the technicians they produce. It also adds to employers' uncertainty about occupational profiles and how to fit them into their firms. Estimates of the size of the job market for the graduates of technical institutes differ by at least one order of magnitude depending on the source. Moreover, in some countries legislation distorts the market by protecting certain employment positions in the civil service for university graduates. The problems in Latin America generally exceed those in Europe in this respect, although they largely parallel those of other countries, such as Greece (Patrinos 1995; Psacharopoulos 1988). By contrast, the community college in the U.S. has often taken pride in its distinctive niche.

---

[4] No harm comes from using the term university for any place that has university in its name. However, we take care to distinguish among the universities' academic leadership and other functions.

Box 3.2. University Research: A Cycle of Mislabeling and Ill-Advised Policy

Many educational authorities believe that universities should have full-time faculty engaged in research. Too often, people with undergraduate degrees (or without degrees) are hired for roles they are unable to perform. They pass on through the ranks without evaluation or with phony or diluted evaluations. The result may be a costly system of extreme *homologación* and corrupt egalitarianism pushing toward gigantic confusion as imaginary academics adopt formalities without corresponding substantive change (Gil 1998:69).

True research in the sense of original work is very rare. Teaching is deprecated as a lower-level task. To clamp down on shirkers, administrators may declare that all those not engaged in research will have to teach more. This, in turn, leads more people to list as research any activity that yields new knowledge to them or any activity that is basically professional practice; research becomes operationally defined as anything that is not classroom teaching. It would be better to restrict the definition and official status of research and to redefine and bolster teaching beyond the classroom to include hours of studying, reading, and thinking.

The second problem occurs when public policy does in fact recognize more than one form of higher education. It then often glorifies and rewards institutions that purportedly, but rarely in fact, perform academic leadership functions. This undermines the other functions of higher education as well as those institutions that truly are academically superior regardless of whether they have the official university nomenclature. Universities often benefit from rights and resources properly associated with only a small part of what they really do. Other institutions are legally but arbitrarily blocked from sources of funding or from granting graduate degrees. These practices lead to perverse stratification. Public policy fails to make distinctions where true differences warrant them and makes too many distinctions where they are not warranted.

Third, perverse policies make it rational for institutions, units, and individuals to act in ways that aggravate the situation. Applying the same treatment to all institutions stifles or distorts competition, obviates evaluation, and removes incentives. For example, the Rockefeller Foundation was frustrated when its early grants aimed at specific units of the University of Chile led to the redistribution of other finance. This situation is replicated wherever funders are stymied in their performance-based giving. In some cases, rewards are reserved for universities or academic leadership activities, making other types of institutions try to fit into those categories. They lobby for formal status and its privileges. For example, higher education in Brazil has suffered when schools have become universities and the students have become *universitarios* whose diplomas have carried legal weight in the job market (Schwartzman 1996b). [5]

Fourth, criticism of universities can diminish their best academic and professional work. We do not want to deprecate, but rather to protect and bolster the region's closest approximations to a university ideal and the legitimate aspirations to build upon those approximations. We argue against the term university if it is sloppily employed and especially against the legal sanctioning that makes false distinctions and creates incentives for the worst sort of mimicry.

In sum, analysis and treatment of higher education focuses too much on universities and on their purported functions more than their real functions. The academic leadership function conventionally associated with the term university remains poorly developed in Latin America. Higher education and even universities mostly do something else. Meanwhile, much of the best academic work (publications, scholarly dialogue and evaluation, and demanding graduate education) takes place outside universities or within exceptional units in universities. It would be helpful to match analysis and policy more closely to reality.

---

[5] This market reserve problem appears to lessen, however, as so many more degree holders compete for jobs.

CHAPTER 4

A TYPOLOGY
FOR DISTINGUISHING
MYTH FROM REALITY

Rather than pretending that all higher education does or should pursue the same ends, we should deal as much as possible with the various functions that higher education does and should fulfill. Only then can we take a major step from myth to reality.

Taking up the research challenge set forth by Schwartzman (1996b), in this chapter we develop a typology of the functions of higher education. The typology is based on four functions—academic leadership, professional development, technological training and development, and general higher education—that are fundamental to the diagnosis and proposed reforms presented in this book. A key policy rationale for the typology is to help improve the performance of each function by applying the most appropriate resources, rules, and incentives. We hope the typology will also be helpful in other regions as well as in individual countries in Latin America.

Tentativeness and certain limitations characterize our typology. Whereas higher education does much socially, culturally, and politically, we specify the typology of functions largely in economically relevant terms and with emphasis on teaching and learning. The functions nevertheless encompass more than particular fields of knowledge or methodologies; they incorporate higher education's commonly identified tasks of teaching, research, and extension (a limited term for the sort of joint efforts, service, and accountability contemplated here). Each of the four functions should define and mix the three tasks differently. In terms of the coverage of the typology, the functions lack mutual exclusiveness. Particular tasks might reasonably fall within more than one category or on the border between categories, or multiple tasks could become intertwined.

Application of the typology will sometimes prove complex, difficult, and debatable; however, even in challenging cases, the typology should provide guidance. The question is not whether the typology can solve all issues, but whether it helps to clarify thinking and improve policy. Another limitation arises when we apply the typology to a real world constructed of institutions that undertake more than one function. The typology should not be rigidly applied with tight a priori rules for several reasons. First, the real world of institutions and actors is too complex. Second, some mixing of functions provides for innovative cross-fertilization. Third, rules that reward a given function may encourage places to attempt what they are not suited to do. Fourth, the U.S. is notorious for sloppy nomenclature, yet it soars to the top in academic leadership, while it allows many academically feeble institutions to call themselves universities.

The difficulties of application do not reflect failures of the typology as much as they reflect the reality of institutions performing several functions and the confusion that develops about which rules and incentives relate to each function. Indeed, most universities try to perform different functions in many of their units or courses. The typology could help delineate functions to which rules conceived for other functions are often wrongly applied. The problem is not inherently the mixing of functions within institutions or even within internal units; indeed, universities sometimes play positive roles in integrating various tasks. Institutions run into problems when they pay insufficient attention to their own functional differentiation.

Policymakers, analysts, and the general public should regard all four functions as essential to modern higher education and its role in national development. It is important to minimize invidious comparisons among the functions. We reject the common tendency to regard academic leadership as the best or highest function and technological training and development or general higher education as the worst or lowest. Instead, the main policy rationale for the typology is to help match performance with appropriate mechanisms, rules, and incentives. What suits one function may be pointless or even detrimental for others. Of course, figuring out the proper matches (let alone implementing them) is not so easy. But it is a more proper challenge than trying to figure out a one-size-fits-all policy.

Three questions require consideration for each of the four functions. First, what is the function? Second, what are the basic needs for it to work well? Third, what is the balance between accomplishments and problems, and what are the key variables that determine that balance?

Academic Leadership

Academic leadership corresponds to most poeple's idea of a university. It involves conventional academic quality, including smart and well-prepared students and professors, and teaching and research distinguished by theoretical or methodological sophistication.

A Home for Intellectuals

Academic leadership includes prestigious undergraduate education, but its most defining aspects are graduate education and research (Clark 1993, 1995; Geiger 1993). The faculty members are intellectual leaders and some of their students will become their successors. The students also will form much of the future political, administrative, business, and cultural leadership. Academia produces the leading critics of the status quo, a point that underscores the centrality of independent thinking in academic work. Those with the most advanced academic training often lead national debates. While most prestigious academic work takes place in the basic and social sciences, it should not be identified solely with these careers. Traditionally, law, engineering, and medicine had this role in Latin America as they employed the intellectually most advanced minds and attracted the intellectually most advanced students.

Although the term academic leadership inevitably speaks to a rather exclusive function and will be politically bothersome to some, it does not denote socioeconomic elitism. Instead, it expresses that a certain kind of teaching and research occurs only where levels of intellectual preparation and funding are unusually high.[1] The academic leadership function accounts for only a small portion of the enrollment in national higher education, even in rich countries. Depending

[1] The term "elite" is used in the comparative higher education literature and indeed we might have labeled the function "academic elite." It would not be altogether bad if the label's political sensitivity scared off some that would like to claim academic vanguard status. The label might thereby help restrict to a few places the generous treatment that academic leadership needs. In any event, even if this portion of higher education is decried as elitist, higher education overall should not be called elitist because most enrollments lie beyond this function.

on definitional rigor, it might characterize only 3 percent of the more than 3,000 higher education institutions in the U.S. The figure rises by including top liberal arts colleges; it falls closer to 1 percent by limiting the count to institutions in which virtually all programs do serious research. By contrast, the academic leadership function accounts for a much larger portion of expenditures on higher education. Costs per student are unavoidably high in institutions that perform the academic leadership function.

Academic leadership provides a good illustration of the general point, valid for all four functions, that higher education goes beyond training and service to students. Academic work contributes to national development through intensive teaching of future leaders, pathbreaking research in sciences and humanities, and guidance of broad segments of society and government.

Needs: A Special and Expensive Diet

Academic leadership has special needs. Mainly, it requires ample resources and autonomy. Research costs more than teaching, graduate education costs more than undergraduate education, and education of high academic quality costs more than most other higher education. Indeed, the costs of academic leadership, like some excellent professional or advanced technological education and research, may make it especially difficult for small, poor countries. To retain the best intellects in the country as teachers, the higher education system must pay more than it would to hire others who are less advanced in scholarship. The government must cover much of the expense because the marketplace does not capture many of the returns. For example, the scholar whose research on genetics helped Brazil to generate billions of dollars annually from soybean production lives on a modest salary.

Academic leadership is the function that most justifies autonomy for higher education. This may be decried as elitist, but truly elite academic undertakings merit the treatment; indeed, they require it. Intellectuals need freedom to develop new, critical, and often unpopular ideas. Their tasks are often arcane and should not be held too directly accountable in the short run to the government, the public, or the market. The worldwide move toward more direct and immediately measurable accountability to government or the public, and the increasing weight of market dynamics that lead to "entrepreneurial universities" (Clark 1998) present dangers as well as benefits. The higher education system must protect intellectuals from the changing winds in these external arenas. It has to protect intellectuals from pressures generated inside universities that mix in other functions or pursue extra-academic political or social agendas. It should protect intellectuals from the sort of massive growth of the higher education system that engulfed Uruguay in 1983 and, more generally, that engulfed Latin America in the 1960s and 1970s.

Consistent with autonomy is the idea that most controls should be internal. Academic leadership must be as accountable as other functions of higher education, but peer assessment provides the key to the accountability of the academic leadership function. External evaluation must complement the procedures and social pressures of the academic ethos (Clark 1983). International standards and comparisons reinforce the open and competitive evaluation of the academic leadership function and do not isolate higher education in an ivory tower. The system can benefit from a blend of peer reviews and external evaluations, as in competitive funding for research. In Paes de Carvalho's terms, too much secure money hypnotizes, while too much volatility traumatizes.

In a country that cannot meet the needs of the academic leadership function, national development suffers in economic, social, cultural, and political terms. The country falls prey to a debilitating brain drain that hurts national development overall.

Performance: Seeking More That Is Real

One performance problem is that Latin America suffers from insufficient academic leadership. This problem is widely recognized, notwithstanding the claims of substantial production by individual universities. Only a few universities in the region remotely resemble the international academic leaders of the world.[2]

This problem is easily exaggerated, given that the academic leadership function should constitute only a small percentage of enrollments. In fact, considerable progress has been made in building academic work in the region. The numbers of well-trained professors,

---

[2] The fact that Latin America does not have institutions to match the University of Tokyo or the University of California-Los Angeles is mostly beside the point. The same might be said for a country like Portugal, where OECD observers have been impressed with the academic level and progress (OECD 1998b).

solid graduate programs, research centers, and well-equipped laboratories are much larger than they were three decades ago. This achievement gets obscured because the overall size of higher education has multiplied and most is not academically advanced.

Another problem is that pretenders hurt the academic leadership function. Even graduate programs in most universities provide less academic excellence and more professional, quasi-professional, or general higher education. The university pretenders make it hard to identify where the real academic leadership function occurs and, with their clamoring for equal treatment, make it hard to give those supplying the real function the special and expensive diet they require. Too little real academic leadership and too much false leadership characterize the system.[3] For instance, it is better for a country to have one first-class academic library with wide access for people outside the university that may house it, than to have many mediocre ones.

The key policy challenge, therefore, is to identify and nurture academic leadership without extending its proper treatment to other functions. National and even regional centers of excellence, with the healthy by-product of promoting inter-American integration, make sense both to expand the core of academic leadership and to curb the number and funding of the poorly prepared aspirants. But the notion that all higher education or even all university institutions are or can be academic leaders is a myth that cripples analysis of both contemporary reality and reasonable reform options.

Professional Development

A second function of higher education is professional development. Although it overlaps academic leadership in some respects, distinctions between the two are significant.

---

[3] Governments in industrial countries are trying to figure out how to target research funds without having them siphoned off into universities' general funds (Clark 1993). Separate institutions or separate structural units inside institutions are common but imperfect answers. Problems include the isolation of advanced academic work from undergraduate learning, an inability to produce the next generation of scholars, and excessive dependence on markets that demand quick, applied research (Levy 1996a:117–22, 201–38). In Latin America, such problems are severe because the mainstream university structures are weak.

Advanced Education Ties Directly to Practice

The professional development function principally prepares students for specific job markets that require advanced and extensive formal education. It enables graduates to apply their expertise to such challenges as treating diseases, designing buildings, or handling legal disputes. In classical terms, the professional function educates medical doctors, dentists, veterinarians, and those engineers, architects, and lawyers whose work directly employs the skills they learned in their programs of study. In recent years, many other professional fields have been created, including computer sciences and modern engineering specialties. They all have in common the transmission of the skills of a well-defined occupation in terms of subject matter and technique. At the same time, some high-level training (such as industrial engineering) leads to a more diffuse job market than seen in traditional medical fields, for example. In Latin America, as in Europe, the professional development function occurs in first-degree or, to use the common U.S. term, undergraduate programs; in the United States, it usually takes place in graduate programs on top of a more general undergraduate program.

Like the academic leadership function, the professional development function is not a mass undertaking. Indeed, it includes a kind of elite education, with a share of the graduates equipped to become social and political elites after their legal, medical, engineering, or other studies. Yet, preparation for professional practice is the immediate and dominant goal and, accordingly, it should shape the professional curriculum.

Not every professional school is or should be very selective. Professional schools vary more than academic leadership schools in the required levels of sophistication for students and professors. A modern society requires a vast number of people with specific skills to perform tasks for which on-the-job learning, self-learning, or improvisation is insufficient. Individuals must spend time in school to learn engineering and advanced computer programming. Professional schools fulfill the important role of providing society with graduates who possess these well-specified skills.

Although the analysis here focuses on the preparation of students for specific job markets, the professional development function goes beyond teaching and into research and extension as well. Good training remains a necessary (though insufficient) condition for research and extension, as those trained professionally carry out much of the research and extension in question. In research, professional development obviously overlaps academic leadership. Professional development emphasizes more the application of research. University extension often means professionals playing concerts, assisting local arts, giving health care or legal advice at reduced or no cost for the poor, and so forth. Thus, professional higher education is properly identified not only with employment slots, but also with the entire range of professional work.

Needs: Driven Largely by the Market

As the main control mechanism required by professional education, the labor market should determine the number of students and the curriculum. Market control is especially important when dealing with expensive training, to avoid costly and disillusioning overproduction. Professional development programs sometimes need to achieve economies of scale, which can be a problem in small or poor countries.

The market need not be fully private; indeed, countries must acknowledge the social utility of professional development beyond pure market value (for example, service to the poor or to the environment). However, most professional training should be driven by economic more than social or political demand. In the professional development function, teachers' pay should be linked to the specific markets for their professions, so that the schools will be able to hire the teachers who are leaders in their fields. The market should further influence the standard of competence, which is not necessarily demonstrated by possession of a diploma. The labor market, more than the wisdom of high-ranking educators, should signal the curriculum and the number of students. Professional education should resist extra-economic pressures for indefinite expansion.[4] But all this leaves ample room for leadership and thoughtful initiatives in higher education. Policymakers should interpret job market signals and, where possible, anticipate emerging job market requirements, rather than react slavishly or belatedly. They should choose among various options, for example, in terms of how to formulate the curriculum.

---

[4] Resistance should be especially firm where outlays are heavy in facilities or personnel. It is less important in fields like law, which are less costly and can lead to diverse and worthwhile employment. And it is less important in the general education function.

Because of the centrality of specific skills for the market, professional education is a good candidate for the individual certification of graduates. Medical board tests, bar examinations, and accounting certifications are obvious examples. An added advantage, such testing allows programs to experiment with their curricula and delivery systems as long as they can arrive at the bottom-line performance standards.

Professional programs should maintain close ties to the professions themselves on an ongoing basis. They can achieve these ties by appointing representative practitioners and employers to governing boards, boards of trustees, and financial boards (*patronatos*). They could also create special advisory committees and steering groups. In cases where professional programs operate in universities that also perform other functions, the input can be structured at the program or school level.[5] The higher education system should include accreditation by professional program, as opposed to just institutional accreditation. Along with extension activities, as in the fine arts or agriculture, such governance ties help bring job-relevant realism, information, and funds from the market. These ties also produce a healthy flow of information, applied research, and graduates from the institutions to the labor market.

An important and complex issue concerns the role of research. To arrive at practical guidelines, policymakers should balance the possibilities and the constraints. The professional function goes beyond training to include the applied research conducted in some of the region's renowned schools. In fact, much research and development takes place in the top engineering and medical schools, and it is an important contribution of higher education. Academic leadership has often emerged within such schools, reflecting the functional mix that can occur within units. Good research deserves encouragement, but schools that prepare competent professionals and professional extension programs do not always require a research component. Professional schools miss the point when they identify research as a basic need and mandate its pursuit. Even excellent teaching schools do not require widespread research, as illustrated by *Grandes Ecoles,* France's institutions of professional education. It is unrealistic to expect research

---

[5] Again, care is required because of the mix of functions within institutions. Business representation on universitywide governing boards can risk subjecting the academic leadership or general education tasks performed within the same institutions to undue intervention by nonacademic professionals.

to be a centerpiece in most competent and serious but not affluent professional schools. In addition, some of the best teachers are practitioners who are unable to do research. Finally, where research is warranted, the need is less often for abstract books than for innovative work that is concrete and practical.

The professional function must not surrender its essence by emulating the academic leadership function. For example, recruitment of faculty with advanced degrees or publications should not come at the cost of whatever professional experience is crucial to training. The good teacher is often the good professional. As a director of an industrial design school put it: "We do not have professional teachers; we have professionals who also teach."

At the same time, many professional schools do well by mixing full-time professional teachers with professional practitioners who usually teach part time. The mix depends on the field, the job market, research and extension, and the level of sophistication. In some cases, the best possible professional education involves incorporating elements most associated with academic leadership or general education. But professional schools should ensure that academic pretensions do not deprecate direct professional training or push aside basic professional needs.

Performance: Steering a Course between Overproduction and Obsolescence

Latin American higher education has carried out professional development much more than academic leadership. It has done so in freestanding programs and in programs within universities. It has produced relevant research and worthy extension in many fields. It has produced the great majority of good professionals by providing ample, concrete knowledge and skills. The gap in professional development between industrial countries and Latin America is much smaller than the gap in academic leadership. Critics of Latin American higher education often ignore or implicitly devalue professional development as they focus on their academic ideals.

Frequently, however, professional education falls prey to the twin problems of loose overproduction and excessive rigidity. Loose overproduction occurs when professional development drifts into quasi-professional education. Excessive rigidity develops when it becomes too isolated, thus hampering basic professional employment and related research and extension activities. At its best, professional development has steered a successful course between the twin problems.

The problem of overproduction means that few of the graduates from professional development schools are really professionals with appropriate skills and knowledge to enter the job market in their field. Many graduates are quasi-professional. Quasi-professional reality is professional myth. Lack of understanding or acceptance of this point leads to anger and debates at cross-purposes. Whereas frustration with the academic leadership function focuses mostly on unrealized dreams, frustration with the professional development function concerns deterioration, for the region's university was traditionally a professional institution. For example, at one time, the region's leading professionals made up the teaching staff of the professional schools. As higher education grew, the percentage of true professionals on staff gave ground to academic experts without professional experience and was dwarfed by recent graduates who had neither practitioner nor academic skills. Similarly, multiplying enrollments have overwhelmed the moderate increases in true professional education by mammoth quasi-professional growth. As a result, many graduates cannot obtain jobs in their chosen field.[6]

To better delineate professional development from the quasi-professional and to otherwise improve performance, Latin America must implement more of the control mechanisms appropriate to professional education. Many programs need to get closer to their professions and their markets. Markets presently have too little influence in the face of sociopolitical demands for the expansion of higher education. As a result, the higher education system wastes resources and loses legitimacy, and state employment rises excessively (so as to avoid political unrest).[7]

The other major problem, excessive rigidity, occurs when professional schools do not get a close fit between what they teach and the

---

[6] Medical programs have probably held up best as truly professional. Solid institutions thrive in other fields as well, for example, in the engineering programs at Mexico's Monterrey Tech and Brazil's ITA São José dos Campos.

[7] There needs to be more testing. The lack of testing is actually a sign of deterioration. When higher education was small, it excluded those without an impressive secondary school background. Higher education had a high percentage of capable instructors. The legal equivalence of a university degree with accreditation (*habilitación*) for practicing a profession made some sense. Now, political pressures for such equivalence are strong and extend to quasi-professions, as a form of protectionism. De facto, employers respond, bypassing provisions regarding rights to employment and instead testing job applicants (Cleaves 1987). But the screening is not as extensive and tight as it needs to be.

specific skills needed in the labor market. Frequently, professional education fails because of obsolete curriculum. The schools need to recognize changes in the workplace and take them into consideration in teaching. Also, the schools should resolve the problem of lack of hands-on experience during training.

From a different perspective, the internationally supported reforms of the 1960s found that higher education was too rigidly professional. Too narrow in its preparation for a particular job, higher education did not open itself sufficiently to science, social science, research, and general studies. One set of deleterious consequences involved the ways in which the professions choked off broader university development (and choked off the other three functions).[8] Another set involved injury to professional education itself. The reformers believed, for example, that graduates could be better lawyers if they studied sociology or ethics. In that case, the teaching staff would need to include sociologists or philosophers rather than just lawyers. It would also need to include professional pedagogues, thinkers (*pensadores*), or wise people (*sabios*) rather than only practitioners teaching part time. Students should take some classes, including electives, with students from other programs and departments. In other words, the programs should be revamped to prepare true professionals rather than narrow professionals or technicians. They should also be revamped to foster relevant research and extension.

In sum, the region's professional higher education must address its twin problems of loose overproduction and excessive rigidity. That will require both more innovative mixes with other functions and more protection of its own particular, market-driven needs. Such protection means a clearer separation from what passes for professional education but is not.

Technological Training and Development

Unlike the professional development function, the technological training and development function is rather new for higher education.

---

[8] Where individual professions controlled the separate programs, the goals of university development and institutionwide reforms proved difficult. These included coherent institutional management, planning, leadership, and construction of campuswide facilities (for example, one university library instead of the uncoordinated string of small, parochial, and partly duplicating ones housed in each program or department).

Most of what fits here either did not previously exist, or was handled at the secondary vocational level or in on-the-job training (Kirberg 1981). It is important to think of the careers here as lifted into higher education rather than as shortened (watered-down, second-class) professional higher education. Table 4.1 shows the number of technological institutions.

Focused Training, Jobs, and More

The technological training and development function provides specific skills for the immediate labor market. The narrowest of the four functions, it provides the least theory and the most practice. However, narrowness does not necessarily imply less importance. And narrowness is a relative term; higher education in technology concerns more than teaching and learning. Applied technological research is vital to national technological development and, through extension, to a better life for many when appropriate technologies are crafted for specific situations. Whereas narrow forms of training may appropriately be labeled "technical," we mostly use the overlapping term technological to subsume and go beyond that activity.

As with each function, many examples fit clearly, whereas others lie ambiguously near a borderline. For example, the technological-professional boundary can blur—although technological work usually lies far from the classic high professional work. In terms of training, short programs that award a degree different from the university degree fit the technological function, but some four-year programs with university degrees probably fit too, in administrative areas bordering on the general higher education function (including some related to tourism, management, or accounting). In any event, the analysis here contemplates mostly skills like x-ray technicians, bookkeeping, physiotherapy, avionics, and electronics. Such skills are learned in community colleges in the United States, in Institutes Universitaires de Technologie in France, and in Fachhochschulen in Germany.

Needs: The Market at the Core—Mostly

Technological training and development requires an even stronger tie to the market than professional development. Because the training is so specific, a mismatch with the market is disabling, whereas a good match puts accumulated information, skills, and attitudes to good ad-

Table 4.1. The Number of Higher Education Institutions, by Type, 1994

Country	Polytechnic institutes and universities			Technological and other institutions			Teacher training institutes			Other institutions	Total
	Public	Private	Total	Public	Private	Total	Public	Private	Total		
Argentina	37	42	79	—	—	—	—	—	—	1,674	1,753
Bolivia[a]	12	23	35	21	—	21	23	2	25	—	81
Brazil	68	59	127	5	10	15	155	349	504	205	851
Chile	25	45	70	—	73	73	—	127	127	—	270
Colombia	51	96	147	16	33	49	—	—	—	62	258
Costa Rica	4	20	24	68	207	275[b]	—	—	—	—	299
Cuba	7	—	7	9	—	9	12	—	12	7	35
Domican Republic	1	24	25	—	6	6	—	—	—	4	35
Ecuador	15	8	23	42	75	117	31	3	34	—	174
El Salvador	2	44	46	15	6	21	2	—	2	4	73
Guatemala	1	5	6	—	1	1	1	1	2	—	9
Honduras	2	4	6	—	1	1	1	—	1	3	11
Mexico	39	49	88	110	—	110	215	111	326	146	670
Nicaragua	4	7[c]	11	1	3	3	—	—	—	—	14
Panama	3	13	16	1	4	5	—	—	—	—	21
Paraguay	3	12	15	—	—	—	23	14	37	20	72
Peru	28	25	53	228	212	440	119	65	184	—	677
Uruguay[a]	1	1	2	—	—	—	3	—	3	16[d]	21
Venezuela	17	15	32	26	16	42	—	1	1	39	114
Total	320	492	812	541	647	1,188	585	673	1,258	2,180	5,438

a. 1995.
b. 176 of these are not recognized by the Ministry of Education.
c. Two of these are private with state aid.
d. One of these has 25 campuses that have not been counted.
Source: García Guadilla (1996b:266).

vantage. Just as performance should be mostly attuned to the market, so should governance and funding mechanisms. In order to fit its market, technological training and development requires employer representation as well as special assistance (for example, research and development). It requires teachers with practical experience and flexibility to adapt to the changing labor market. Technological schools in Germany and other European countries have done well in including industry representatives on their governing boards. These representatives have pushed for short, practical courses of study. Appropriate governance also means the schools have the institutional autonomy to change course contents and offerings, as well as some financial autonomy to buy and sell courses, services, supplies, and equipment. Overall, labor market controls should be powerful enough to limit other control mechanisms, although there is a place for testing and certification.[9]

The need for rapid responsiveness in the technology function is unmatched in any other function. A fast-changing job market requires a fast-changing and specific curriculum. The schools must frequently overhaul their programs and continually add new disciplines. When telephones become cellular, technicians must study cellular telephone technology; when computer aided design/computer aided manufacturing (CAD/CAM) specifications are transmitted by satellite, courses have to adjust.

Like its professional development counterpart, technological training and development sometimes requires heavy outlays, sometimes not. Shorter courses naturally tend to be cheaper, but costs depend on the field in question and the intensity of use of facilities. That intensity depends, in turn, on the width of markets: wide ones allow for intensive use of teachers and equipment, yielding low costs per student. Small and poor countries may have trouble due to the limited size of their markets for these multiple specialized degrees.

The idea of the market at the core makes sense insofar as the focus is on training. Greater analysis of technological research and development would have to delineate where the market is properly joined with or even subordinated to the needs or goals of the state, nongovernmental organizations, or other interests.

---

[9] The testing should be easy and sensible to administer. Fields like avionics and some electronics need national tests based on domestic or even international standards. Europe has a long tradition, increasingly emulated elsewhere, of certification for an array of technical jobs.

Performance: Big Is Beautiful

The lack of research on technological training and development in higher education makes it difficult to assess performance.[10] Analysts need more information to distinguish this function appropriately from related professional activities. They also need to know much more about the market's disposition to hire graduates of technological training and development schools as opposed to providing more on-the-job training. And they need more evidence on how well technological higher education works for graduates and society. The more developed literature on vocational secondary education has raised serious doubts about what works and has stimulated further research on the factors that would lead to better performance.

The available evidence indicates that technological higher education is larger than expected, given most discussions of higher education policy and the stereotype of an unchanging or monolithic higher education system. For example, Argentina's Technological University has 55,000 students, 9 percent of the university total. The institution differs significantly from the national university in terms of student background, emphasis on applied research, and fields of study (Mollis 1995). Panama's technological university has roughly 10,000 students.

Most nations have established a formal sector within the higher education system that at least comes closer to meeting the needs for technological training and development than universities do. In other cases, universities have added short programs in technology to their mix of offerings. In Mexico, some authorities have demonstrated their appreciation of the possibilities of expanding higher education through nontraditional options. Because of the inadequacies in its pre-existing network of regional technological institutes and agricultural institutes, the country has recently established two-year institutions that mimic community colleges in the United States. The Mexican institutions have ties to the workplace and to employers who sit on boards and influence curriculum design. Brazil has established several Federal Training Centers (CEFETs) and 18 National Service of Industrial Learning (SENAI) technical centers. Chile's training centers show the increasing weight of private sector courses with inter-institutional competition

---

[10] Assessments of the inadequacy of technological research in Latin America and what might be done about it sometimes deal simultaneously with science and technology. See, for example, Mayorga (1997).

and aggressive marketing (Courard 1992). Peru also has a sizable private technological sector. Costa Rica has made progress with some of its parauniversities, institutions offering programs that are shorter than those of universities (Hodges 1993).

Although several countries have made progress, most still have far too little technological training and development in proportion to the overall higher education system. Disdain for manual labor, the prestige of professional education, aspirations to academic leadership status, and legal privileges for the professional development and academic leadership functions have hurt technological training and development (Safford 1976). Attempts to expand or control technological training and development have gone awry because they were based on a priori beliefs more than on trial-and-error in reading market signals. Many intermediate degrees are not true short-cycle programs with identifiable value in the job market. The fact that more students do not flock to technological training and development programs probably suggests that they have weak rates of return relative to other types of higher education (Bracho and Padua 1995).

In general, technological training and development copies other higher education too much. The most common error in designing its courses is constructing miniature forms of regular engineering programs. Curricula become short versions of their four- or six-year counterparts. This design produces weaker courses, with little comparative advantage vis-à-vis the long programs. A related problem is that the courses have too much theory and not enough practice. For example, when the shorter programs must teach the theoretical beginnings of French-inspired engineering, they have little time left for practical exploration of technology and hands-on applications. Even where separate sectors are formally established for technological training and development, the pressure to gain the status of their professional and university counterparts often leads to "academic drift." This is a common tendency internationally and sometimes, as in Great Britain, the "binary" system of separate university and technological sectors is formally undone. Latin America needs more study of both its own and international examples where technological training and development has worked well.[11]

---

[11] See, for example, Meek et al. (1996) for international examples in which technological training copies other forms of higher education. Chile's State Technical University was born from a linking of technical institutions previously not considered higher education. For decades Chile

Latin America has achieved important gains in technological training and development. But it probably has not moved enough in enrollments and surely not nearly enough in accordance with the characteristics and controls appropriate to this particular function.

General Higher Education

The general higher education function has generated the most confusion. It makes up the largest segment of higher education in terms of the number of students.

General Higher Education by Default

There is a common form of higher education in Latin America in which a professional diploma does not lead to a profession, but to a broad range of unspecified and unanticipated jobs. This need not be simply a negative phenomenon; a point advanced by our use of the term general higher education. First, except where it exists in its most deplorable form, general higher education usually leads to gains in employment, not (as commonly asserted) to unemployment. Second, where done well, it carries important benefits beyond those of the immediate marketplace. Through general higher education, countries can build a modern society that is more informed, capable, participatory, cultured, and democratic.

Analysts, policymakers, and the institutions themselves seldom correctly identify the general higher education function. Often, the education in question passes itself off as fulfilling only the other functions, usually the professional development one. Here myth based on false aspirations or self-promotion ultimately proves self-defeating. Judged by its performance in its claimed functions, the general higher education function is often nonfunctional. But judged by what it really

---

had a national technical university as well as the National University of Chile. In the 1970s the technical university was converted into the University of Santiago. Chile has created institutes and raised training centers to a higher education status, while treating the three sectors differently. Among international cases that might be instructive for Latin America, the OECD (1998b) report on Portugal suggests at least some early success with technological universities. Some U.S. community colleges show how technical courses are often at their best when they offer more exposure to practice than regular engineering in absolute terms, and when they apply basic sciences to the concrete context of the occupations.

does, or can do, general higher education provides a sort of worth-while, additional education.

The purpose of identifying this fourth function of higher education is not to give credibility to anything-goes policy or to the poor quality often found. Instead, we want to acknowledge the existence of this function, identify its strong points and weaknesses, and figure out how to make the function more worthwhile. Much improvement is possible.

Although general higher education accurately describes the positive function that should sit respectably alongside academic leadership, professional development, and technological training and development, the term quasi-professional describes much of what really goes on. The quasi-professional represents the failure of the professional. By the 1960s, booming enrollments in many fields (for example, economics, business, law, psychology, architecture, and journalism) produced more job candidates than the market could handle.[12] Professional education thus was deprofessionalized. Spared from the extremes of accelerated expansion were those careers that require significant fixed expenditures to set up (medicine, dentistry, and some subfields in engineering).

The boom in enrollments saturated the market for graduates in most traditional fields as well as in many new fields. In some countries, institutions of higher education have produced ten to twenty times the number of economists and sociologists needed to fill new positions requiring these diplomas. As a consequence, much of higher education has become just four or five years of additional schooling. It remains a professional education in curriculum, structure, legal trappings, and employment goals, but students cannot find jobs corresponding to their sought-after diplomas and they may take up whatever jobs they can find.[13]

Numerically, newer fields account for most of the quasi-professional or general higher education. Traditional fields have grown in ab-

[12] Many Peruvians reportedly guess that only about 10 percent of graduates work in their field, while one expert believes that 40 percent may be a more accurate guess (Arregui 1994); what is evident is that the situation is unclear and that quasi-professional education is quite widespread.

[13] The demise of the traditional fit between study and job has occurred worldwide. Perhaps Latin America's closest parallel lies with Mediterranean countries. Africa's woes involve a much smaller higher education system. Western European and Asian economies have been able to accommodate more growth. In the U.S., the liberal arts orientation makes the disjuncture between study and job more acceptable. Philosophy and biology majors do not automatically expect to be employed as philosophers and biologists. Latin America usually attempts to treat virtually every field of study as a profession.

solute but not proportional terms. The newer fields are mostly business and administration (accounting, business administration, commercial relations, industrial relations, and information management). Teacher training is a mixed, borderline case, handled differently in each country and often elevated into higher education where it provides weak education, mostly for women (see table 4.1 for figures on teacher training institutes). Unlike the traditional fields, the new ones have more inspiration from the United States than from Europe; they tend to debut and flourish especially in private institutions. For example, in business and administration fields, private schools have proportionally twice as many enrollments as public schools. Business and administration fields constitute major growth fields even for the public sector and the largest fields for higher education overall (Levy 1986:265–71, 355).

General higher education in Latin American institutions has limited parallels to colleges in the United States. Quasi-professional education in Latin America has not been designed as a liberal arts education. In U.S. colleges, liberal arts students take a range of courses, usually including elective courses, to broaden their horizons and acquire general knowledge and thinking skills more than specialized knowledge and skills. Instead, the roots and design for Latin America's quasi-professional education lie in professional education in Europe and Latin America. The region's universities rarely pursue true liberal arts as an alternative in the face of mounting evidence of deprofessionalization, that is to say, failure to maintain prior professional goals and standards. On paper, quasi-professional education looks a lot like professional education, but it differs in reality.

In some large universities, in some areas, expansion has kept track with demand, thereby preserving the professional nature of higher education. At the same time, other areas have expanded regardless of the availability of jobs requiring the specific skills of the diploma. When a career becomes deprofessionalized, it should be treated differently. There is nothing inherently wrong with these areas of study if we identify them correctly and implement reform so that they can realistically perform well.

Needs: General Higher Education by Design

As it fails in its professional aspirations, quasi-professional education offers general higher education by default. Latin America needs instead to substitute much more general higher education by design. Although the needs of this component of higher education are dis-

Box 4.1. A Visual Depiction of the Deprofessionalization of Higher Education

Figure A illustrates a traditional model of education. Among the secondary students who proceed directly to the job market, those in technical programs assume technical occupations. Those in academic programs find occupations (often in the service sector) requiring more than primary education, but specific skills can be learned through work experience. Other students from each track obtain degrees that allow entry into higher education (some countries have entrance tests), which concentrates on professions that lead to corresponding jobs (for example, in law or engineering). This remains the basic model under which most public policy is designed. However well it worked for many years, graduates at all levels have come to largely outpace labor market expansion and the neat assumptions of this model are breaking down.

Figure B shows what happens when graduates cannot find jobs related to their education, but their professional degrees help them get better employment than that gained by those who do not have higher education. The graduates take over much of the market for clerical occupations previously supplied by secondary school graduates. Meanwhile, because higher education degrees pay off, many graduates

A. Traditional Model of Education

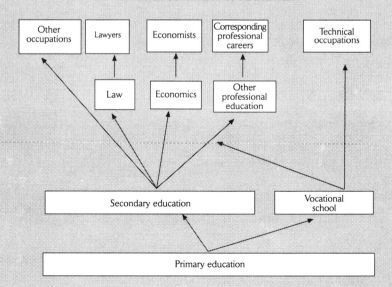

(continued on next page)

Box 4.1. Deprofessionalization *(continued)*

of technical schools disregard their technical skills and try to use their degrees to enter higher education. Some fail because their secondary schools were too weak to prepare them to compete for university entry or success. In other cases, technical schools become a cumbersome way to move through schooling (usually in public institutions, at public expense) to the workplace.

Figure C shows two possible solutions to the problem of deprofessionalization, each already occurring but in need of more recognition and appropriate public policy. The two options introduce quasi-professional (or, we hope, general higher education) and short post-secondary programs into the traditional model of education. The first option is depicted by the addition of the rectangle for general higher education. Professional diplomas still have their markets—after all, a cardiologist must have studied medicine—but new careers and courses that are less professional also blossom, while even the traditional ones "over-produce" for their given fields. Regardless of whether they include a major area of concentration, deprofessionalized programs should

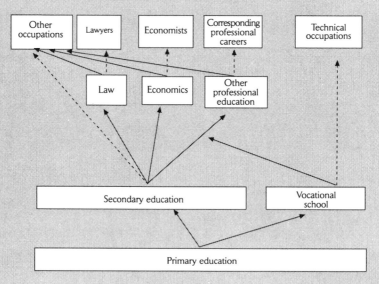

B. Deprofessionalization of Higher Education

Box 4.1. *(continued)*

develop basic or generic skills in writing, reading, mathematics, and problem solving. They respond to a market—largely in clerical, managerial, and service-sector occupations—that wants general skills, not skills that fit a particular occupation. At their best, the new offerings also respond to broader humanistic, cultural, social, and political rationales for a more educated citizenry.

The second option is depicted by the rectangle for short post-secondary programs. It elevates technical occupations to the post-secondary level, as has been done with associate degrees at community colleges in the United States, diplomas at polytechnics (now, university colleges) in the United Kingdom, and parallel forms in other industrial countries. Secondary programs would cease to carry the burden of technical or vocational skills that are not wanted by the students. Students should enroll in this post-secondary option because they seek technical skills for particular labor markets. These courses grow faster than conventional four-year courses in industrial countries and, as the examples of Argentina and Chile suggest, could well do likewise throughout Latin America.

C. Solutions to the Problem of Deprofessionalization

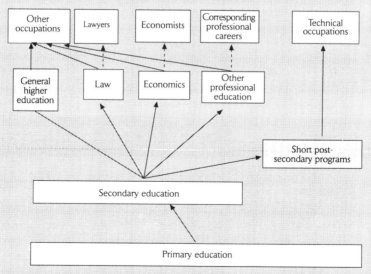

tinctive, they are rarely identified and pursued. General higher education is a worthy function that must be explicitly developed.

Institutions should design general higher education to improve knowledge, thinking, and citizenship. General education should help teach students how to learn and it should help build character. In Europe, for instance, these were long functions of academic secondary schools, leaving higher education free for professional activities. While that system worked earlier in the twentieth century for the small number of students catered to by Latin America's exclusive secondary schools, the majority of students now entering higher education in the region lack such background. In fact, by the 1950s and 1960s, reformers recognized the value of general higher education and pushed for general studies and basic cycles.

In addition, the higher education system needs more texts, more open discussion, and more writing exercises in place of passive note taking from dry lectures. Many policies that may be defended for professional studies (for example, lock-step curricula or courses in sociology given by engineers) make much less sense for quasi-professional students who will work in diverse areas, with graduates from diverse educational backgrounds. One egregious example of rigidity is that students deep into their quasi-professional (or professional) program often cannot switch programs without starting all over again. Professional forms that are too rigid for the purposes of general higher education must yield to much more flexible forms.

Even though the purpose of general higher education is not limited to the job market, it is relevant to the job market. Employers increasingly demand higher education degrees. The crux of the matter here is that general higher education is appropriate, or must make itself appropriate, where employers demand not a particular professional degree but rather any degree or any of a range of degrees.

It follows that general higher education needs its own set of control mechanisms. It does not need market judgments that rest on direct placement into specific jobs. It does not need the sort of peer review associated with academic leadership. Instead, for general higher education, institutional accreditation should judiciously adapt to certain market and peer review measures.[14] Evaluators could also use

---

[14] Longer-term follow-up studies of employment after general higher education could be helpful (allowing, however, that one cannot make the same causal inferences between higher education received and job held that exist for specific types of professional or technological educa-

tests of student knowledge. However, it is more difficult to measure the intellectual growth pursued by general higher education than the specific knowledge and skills pursued by professional and technological education. Other forms of public regulation may be desirable as well.

With its priority of undergraduate teaching, general higher education rarely requires large per capita expenditures. Moreover, public expenditures can be especially small; private institutions (with their incentives to keep expenditures low) already hold much of these enrollments and could hold more, and loans could partly replace subsidies for enrollments in public institutions.

Another reason for low per capita expenditures is that—unlike academic leadership—general higher education is not centrally about research. It emphasizes the transmission of knowledge more than the discovery of knowledge. Research could complement general higher education and bring enriched perspectives to teachers and students. But, given the practical realities of scant research, scarce resources, and the very modest levels of academic preparation that characterize the mass of teachers and students, general higher education does not require research as a necessary core activity (Gil 1994). Instead of pretending that general higher education can emulate on a mass scale what academic leadership does, attention should turn to cost-effective ways to inject relevant modes of research, analysis, and findings into teaching. For example, researchers could run seminars for teachers and help to revamp curricula. Many liberal arts colleges in the United States show an appropriate emphasis on teaching over research; they also indicate how to inject the benefits of research once the institutions attain a certain level of academic credibility and professionalism.[15]

General higher education in particular can use diverse means of instruction (such as correspondence, radio, television, and computers) that in effect link to extension programs as well as to teaching. New instructional mediums offer opportunities to reach students who oth-

---

tion). However, some justification exists for academic self-rule, but less than in the leadership function, and there is less academic ethos and expertise to rely upon.

[15] As general education inches toward academic leadership in undergraduate education, expenditures for staff and programs increase. For example, an increased proportion of full-time staff with at least some advanced academic training may be warranted. At that point, the infusion of more research methods and substance into teaching becomes more feasible. But the integration of research and teaching must be adapted to contexts that differ from those typically looked at by its leading proponents in the developed world, such as Clark (1997).

erwise would remain without a post-secondary educational option. These new means, however, need to overcome public suspicion, criticism from interest groups, and ideological enemies. Therefore, they have to start well, with the backing of solid and reputable organizational structures. Otherwise, they will not avoid the fate of the technically successful but politically weak initiatives undertaken in the past.

Quasi-professional education cannot become general higher education by design overnight. It cannot make a massive transformation into liberal arts. But many institutions can achieve the goals of general higher education. A strategy for improvement can start by identifying what is sound or promising in the performance of the general higher education function to date.

Performance: What Is Worthwhile?

Performance varies across the wide terrain of general higher education. Performance excels where it imparts a truly broadening education, building students' knowledge and analytical abilities. At worst, it fails in its attempts to produce professional development, academic leadership, or technological training.

What are the appropriate criteria for judging performance? Much of general higher education occurs in the private sector and it seems unlikely that hundreds of thousands of students would pay the full or near full cost of quasi-professional studies in return for nothing.[16] In the face of legitimate worries about low quality, however, the basic criterion for judgment should be value added. Does general higher education give students something worthwhile (relative to the costs)? Students may receive job-related gains despite the absence of job-specific skills. Improved ability to think, put ideas into context, read, write, and calculate should lead to improved job performance or the attainment of better jobs. Rates of return suggest a more positive performance in this respect than common critiques would suggest.[17] By

---

[16] We are being conservative by saying hundreds of thousands of students. The region's private enrollments are close to three million. More are in some sort of quasi- or general higher education, where all or almost all costs are covered by tuition, than in academic leadership, professional development, and technological training.

[17] Graduates earn more than dropouts, who, in turn, earn more than those who do not receive a higher education. More research is needed to compare those who marginally enter higher education, on its quasi-professional side, with those who fall marginally short of access (not to a mass of nonenrollees that includes many who never finish primary school). Our guess, consis-

dealing with ideas and books for four or five years, students improve their knowledge and critical thinking abilities. These skills represent a worthy personal consumption good and a sociopolitical good. General higher education can make an important contribution to a broader platform of informed citizen participation in Latin America's democratic development. General higher education fosters these desirable ends by promoting citizenship, culture, and tolerance. Hard evidence is almost nonexistent, but pioneering before-and-after studies at least indicate growth in knowledge and ability (Muñoz Izquierdo et al. 1995; Martínez 1997).[18]

Many private and public institutions impart almost nothing of value. Riddled with shoddy and even scandalous practices, some institutions do not require students to work or learn, and do not require professors to show up for classes or do more than recite outdated notes. These practices distort the general higher education function; they are not inherent features of general higher education. A great deal of difference separates poor performance from adequate and good performance. Some departments and general studies programs break from professional rigidity. Some traditional and newer programs maintain professional form yet bolster students' analytical skills through their well-structured disciplines. For example, law, theology, and physics offer these benefits when they are taught well.[19]

Quasi-professional performance is crippled by the portion that is nearly valueless or, at best, of very limited value. Improved performance will require curbing the size of this portion and changing it

---

tent with U.S. higher education studies, is that the gain in income is much smaller than the average difference between those with and without higher education. In addition, it is likely that individual rates of return could be attractive based more on credentials than on true gains in knowledge and skills; that would leave general higher education as a worthwhile individual investment but a dubious public one.

[18] The analysis by Muñoz Izquierdo et al. (1995) finds gains in basic thinking, analytical, reading, and mathematical skills. Gains occur in fields that appear to be partly professional and mostly quasi-professional, more so in the social than the technological fields, and more so for students of modest background in a public university (but one that is unusually well governed) than for wealthier students at a private university. The private students finish ahead of the public ones but with less of a lead than existed upon entry to higher education. Most importantly, both groups make significant advances.

[19] Economics is another example. By the early 1970s only 3 percent of graduates from even a leading economics school in Brazil obtained posts as professional economists per se, as defined by a panel of eminent national economists, but many had rewarding jobs (Castro 1970). Arregui (1994:24) finds that many Peruvians working outside their field of study match the income of those working in their field.

where possible through regulations or incentives. As it stands, it is a questionable target for individuals' expenditures and very dubious or unjustifiable for governments'. For the better quasi-professional work, however, judgment of performance depends on costs: where costs are low, and especially where they are borne by the student (with loans), even modest payoffs probably mark a worthwhile performance.

For a more promising future, quasi-professional programs could impart better general higher education by changing the curriculum content. In those programs where only a small proportion of graduates are able to find jobs in the specific occupations for which they train, it would be better to try to maximize the "learning to learn" dimensions of the course of study. Adding more general disciplines may do this. It almost surely requires more critical reading, written reports, problem solving, and individual projects.

Given its unmatched size, quasi-professional or general higher education is crucial to the performance of higher education overall. Most of the truly terrible performance occurs in this function. However, considerable positive activity occurs and much can be done to enhance it. Institutions could offer reasonable programs at reasonable cost, affordable to many students who graduate from secondary schools. What has too often been problematic mass higher education can become quite worthwhile mass higher education.

The Four Functions of Higher Education: A Summary

Table 4.2 provides a sketch of the four functions of higher education. It defines each function, summarizes its needs, and outlines its usual performance. The table should help drive home the need for internal rules that accommodate and promote good performance in the different functions. It should also reinforce the same point for institutions that undertake more than one function, as is the case for those that hold the bulk of the region's enrollments and absorb the bulk of the funding.

Table 4.2. The Four Functions of Higher Education

Function	Definition	Needs	Performance
Academic leadership	• Provides high-quality research, teaching, and extension according to conventional international academic norms • Trains intellectual leaders	• Substantial public funding with a minimum of direct and invasive external control • Autonomy • Peer-based evaluation	• Too little of it, but more than formerly • Occurs both within and outside universities • Poorly delineated from other functions and inadequately protected within multifunctional institutions
Professional development	• Prepares students for specific job markets requiring advanced formal education • Provides related tasks in research and extension	• Governance and funding mechanisms largely labor market oriented, including ties to professional associations • Individual certification • Teachers sometimes need more practical experience than sophisticated academic education	• Traditional strength of the region's higher education • Drift into quasi-professional • Prone to rigidity and narrowness • Obsolete curriculum • Some model extension programs and good applied research
Technological training and development	• Provides short programs of practical skills-based training for middle-level positions in the labor market and, with pertinent research, for a nation's technological development	• Governance and funding mechanisms primarily labor market oriented • Flexible management and curriculum	• Expanding, but too small as a proportion of the whole system • Tendency to mimic conventional higher education • Insufficient practice built into curriculum and insufficient research for national development
General higher education	• Quasi-professional education copies professional modes in teaching; however, the labor market is saturated or ill defined • Sound general education broadens students' horizons and enhances their basic critical abilities	• Modest unit costs • Value added, along with efficiency, is key concept of quality • Accreditation has major regulatory role	• Much is low quality and some value added rarely means sufficient value added • Programs would be much more useful if designed for general higher education

CHAPTER 5

KEY POLICY ISSUES

Three issues are crucial to the performance of higher education in Latin America: public subsidization; incentives, finance, and governance; and tools for quality enhancement and control. For each issue, the four functions have problems, progress already made or underway, and potential for further reform.

Public policy in general could be better attuned to the four functions by avoiding the tendency (in both defenses and criticisms of higher education) to use criteria across the functional board in assessing reality and drawing policy conclusions. However, the discussion on reform should not revolve exclusively or rigidly around the four functions because it is often hard to isolate them in practice.

Public Subsidization of Higher Education

Probably no public policy issue in higher education in Latin America and beyond is presently more hotly debated than subsidization. What, then, does our basic analysis suggest regarding this issue?

Too Inequitable and Indiscriminate

Excessive public subsidization is a problem in Latin American higher education largely because it is too inequitable and indiscriminate (the next section argues that it also distorts incentives and governance). On this issue, we find it particularly important to distinguish our arguments from those made by hard-line opponents of subsidization; in the process, we distinguish our arguments from the extreme stereotypical view of funding reform that is often painted by defenders of the status quo. Indeed, an inelegant but fuller title for this subsection might be "too inequitable and indiscriminate—but not nearly as much as often claimed."

Most economists who specialize in higher education or work in international agencies favor various forms of cost recovery, partly to replace public subsidies (Johnstone 1991; Psacharopoulos 1980; World Bank 1994). Although this book joins in advocating greater privatization of certain kinds, it does not take the position that privatization, even in finance, is always better. It does not advocate the total replacement of public authority by economic markets, and it does support targeted and selected mechanisms of public funding. Furthermore, while the book takes the position that governments presently account for too great a proportion of higher education's income, it does not take the position that the absolute level of government support should fall.

Public subsidization means that the many fund the few and the less affluent subsidize the more affluent. A popular myth charges that the poor pay for the rich. Another myth claims that greater subsidization equals greater progressiveness. In fact, high-income students are a minority and they disproportionately attend unsubsidized or minimally subsidized private universities. Moreover, the truly poor carry a low proportion of the tax load. Most academic studies indicate that approximately 85 to 90 percent of public university students come from the middle class, at least in the region's more developed nations.[1]

In Brazil, fewer than 15 percent of students in higher education come from families in which the father works as a manual laborer. Peasants and indigenous groups have still less access to higher education. For these groups, finishing primary school is the more relevant goal. In Latin America, a region notorious for its income inequality, only about 15 percent of all children make it to the ninth grade (IDB 1998). Thus, without minimizing the mobility achieved by many individuals, public policy must face the fact that a relatively privileged minority receives the bulk of the consumption and investment benefits that higher education provides. Yet, those beneficiaries usually pay either no tuition or minimal tuition. A World Bank study suggests that Latin American students could pay an average of 25 to 30 per-

---

[1] Brunner (1996) and Lomnitz, Mayer, and Rees (1983) cite several sources on the composition of the middle class and on which groups receive subsidies. The view that universities lift the less privileged to the other side of the fence has some merit. It loses steam, however, to the extent that the queue effect operates. Public university rectors earnestly cite data on the percentage of their students who are the first in their family's history to attend higher education. Yet, that is a given when cohort enrollment is much higher than it was a generation ago. And while partisans of expansion may say that equity should be achieved by raising enrollments, such growth would make inequitable subsidies even larger (if less inequitable on average).

cent of the per student cost of public higher education (World Bank 1994:45).

The inequity in higher education looms large against the backdrop of basic education. Latin America performs dismally by international standards in basic education (Castro and Carnoy 1997; Birdsall and Foster 1994), even controlling for the level of economic development.[2] Latin America spends too little on primary education. The fact that some countries have per student costs more than 30 times greater in higher education than in primary education warrants serious attention.

A more general problem is that not all things of value warrant subsidization. Societies must prioritize limited public funds for necessary activities that lack alternative financing. Higher education that can be well fueled without subsidies is not necessarily less important than subsidized higher education. Nor should the case against subsidies be construed as one against large or growing higher education. Policy can simultaneously favor increased enrollments and decreased public shares of the funding to pay for them.

Two types of arguments against any attack on public subsidies need to be appreciated, however. First, inequities are not as large and horrifying as critics often portray. Second, subsidization is warranted for certain purposes, some involving equity, some not. The following factors limit the inequities.

- Tuition finances the private sector much more than subsidies, and the private sector reaches almost 40 percent of Latin American students (see table 2.3).
- The public university has a heterogeneous student body, mostly middle class and fairly modest in socioeconomic background, not largely upper class. Reduced public subsidies could lead to a less diverse student body, depending on how loans work out in practice.
- It is unclear how much subsidization "robs" finance from primary or secondary education. Even if higher education takes

---

[2] Latin American students display learning levels equivalent to those of Southeast Asian and European students with several years less education. An International Educational Assessment study of reading literacy in the late 1980s found Venezuela last among 27 countries; shortly thereafter, students from São Paulo and Fortaleza scored far below students from Asia's newly industrialized countries in mathematics and science, and recent studies of several Latin American nations confirm that sad story.

too large a share of the education budget, overall educational expenditures could be too high or too low.[3]

- It is not clear that alternatives to public spending on higher education would be more equitable. Their effects depend on the particular alternatives and on the government's disposition to fund those alternatives.

- Higher education's inequities are not a major cause of the small representation of the poor in universities, unless we assume that the funds used for higher education would be successfully applied to improving the performance of the poor at lower levels and, thereby, increasing their access to higher education. This is a feasible but unproved hypothesis. At the same time, higher education's service to the underprivileged should not be measured only by the socioeconomic composition of its enrollments.

- In any event, notwithstanding certain populist beliefs, higher education's contribution to society does not center on equity. Society's direct pursuit of greater equality must take place mostly outside higher education.[4]

The higher education system can limit inequities by adopting policies that contribute to equity within its own walls and that justify public subsidies. The system could award scholarships and other compensatory assistance for less privileged students who manage to make their way through secondary studies. In addition, the system could provide loans on reasonably attractive terms for those whose rightful access might otherwise be imperiled by the imposition of tuition. Although defenders of the status quo routinely ignore the fact, scholars and international agencies that advocate public tuition also advocate

---

[3] A common critique is that Latin America stands out as a region that spends lavishly on higher education at the expense of lower education. Actually, Latin America's expenditures per higher education student are low compared with other regions. The ratio of higher education to total education expenditures (or to gross national product) is lower in Latin America than in the United States or Canada. Whether Latin America still spends too much (given the lack of research and the lack of quality in Latin America), whether overall spending on education is sufficient, and whether much of the savings from reduced higher education subsidization would flow to other levels of education are all valid questions that complicate the debate.

[4] This reality goes against equity claims raised by both critics, who think higher education could do much more with better financial policy, and defenders, who think higher education already works for equity and could do more through extension of present policy (for example, by expanding subsidized enrollments).

student loans. We do not believe in tuition-based cost recovery across the board. We believe the system should collect payments from those students who can afford it, make loans available for most students, and provide scholarships for some. There are good arguments for loans to be portable, whether repayment is fixed or based on income, but the system should protect against their use at the worst institutions (Albrecht and Ziderman 1992). Public policy could also assist students in private institutions or evening courses. Special attention might go to poor regions, guarding that public money does not go principally to help the well-to-do who live in those regions.

Public finance is warranted where higher education helps equity by creating a strong positive influence on lower education (Schiefelbein 1985; Clark 1985). For example, it should fund good teacher training, teaching materials, and textbook development. Similarly, some institutions engage in other public services that reach the underprivileged in social welfare matters beyond education per se, such as running hospitals or cultural programs. Higher education can and must serve the underprivileged through its graduates, research, and extension.

To this point, we have disassociated ourselves from the generalized, extreme, anti-subsidy case because we make a moderate and qualified critique of higher education's record on equity. We also object to the general anti-subsidy case because, as we now argue, subsidization makes sense where higher education produces public goods, regardless of the concerns about equity.

On the one hand, we believe that policy in Latin America often indiscriminately subsidizes higher education. That is, the public pays even where the benefits accrue largely to individuals or other particular entities that should pay. On the other hand, a major qualification arises regarding public goods. Thus, we do not argue simply for or against public subsidization, but rather for more discrimination. Governments should concentrate subsidies more on those parts of higher education that have a strong public goods argument.

The need for heavy outlays for long-term investment makes certain important higher educational expenditures unattractive to private actors. Higher education produces ample external economies that are not captured by wages. The scientists who developed hybrid corn did not get paid for the benefits to society, nor could they possibly have individually afforded the education they had received. A similar analysis applies for political leaders who help build democratic stability or entrepreneurs who create jobs and opportunities.

Clearly, science and technology should receive subsidies. Except in limited cases of applied research that brings direct and predictable benefits for firms or other private users (for example, nongovernmental organizations), research will not take place unless public funds pay for it. This argument does not imply that merely inflating the budgets of higher education institutions will produce worthwhile research. Ample experience shows the need for more targeted mechanisms.

The justification for subsidies increases with the increase in policies that promote equity or public goods. Latin American higher education may already post favorable social rates of return. Schiefelbein (1996) reports a rate of 12.3 percent. Obviously, high social rates of return help justify public subsidization. Bennell (1995) pointedly disputes claims that higher education suffers from a big gap between social and private rates or that its rates of return overall stack up poorly against rates produced by lower education. Because Bennell writes about developing countries, it is important to note that these two points apply specifically to Latin America. Moreover, whatever social-private gap may exist in Latin America appears to come mostly from Colombia, Brazil, and Chile—three countries that have large private sectors, a characteristic that presumably reduces the private-social gap in returns. Birdsall (1996) notes that higher education's social rate of return is often underestimated for lack of measurement of what it does beyond undergraduate training. Moreover, inefficiency and excess subsidies, more than anything inherent in higher education, cause low returns.[5]

In short, there is no clear case against all public subsidization of higher education. Sound public goods arguments favor subsidization, including appropriately increased subsidies. Additionally, notwithstanding a powerful negative myth, equity considerations are not huge, obvious negatives. Total cost recovery is therefore not warranted. Increased cost recovery would not provide a cure-all for higher education, and it is wrong to make it a precondition for authorization of international loans or other assistance for reform. Policymakers and

---

[5] Bennell believes that the data fueling the case against higher education subsidies are weak. His analysis of the World Bank's (1995) report finds much of the data old, inconsistent, or otherwise shoddy, and wildly variable among countries within the same region (which should restrain generalizations about regions). Bennell also argues that the analysts selectively interpreted or simply misinterpreted the data. For more on social rates of return, see Birdsall (1996), Bracho and Padua (1995), and Bracho and Zamudio (1994). For more on possible exaggerations in the cost recovery case, see Colclough (1995) and Buchert and King (1995).

international agencies must remember that most of the world has for some time relied overwhelmingly on public subsidies for higher education, with only limited additional resources (Johnstone 1986).

Our rejection of an extreme cost-recovery case does not constitute endorsement of the status quo. We hope that citizens and the policymakers charged to serve them will become more discriminating about the sort of higher education that merits the taxpayers' money. Latin America should turn away from its overly general reliance on public subsidies.

Progress: Diversification in Funding Sources

Immediate campaigns to move from overreliance on annual public subsidization toward healthier revenue diversification must not be too grandiose. Extreme reforms would face strong political opposition. A less noted point is that considerable progress is already underway.

Proposals to impose tuition charges have put many ministers of education in jeopardy in Europe as well as in Latin America. Indeed, the vociferous and effective opposition reflects a political responsiveness (however inequitable for its tilt to middle over lower classes) that places Latin America apart from many of the Asian countries with which it has often been unfavorably compared. A strategy that simply ignores this opposition or attacks it frontally is not wise. Some people want the system to suddenly impose tuition. They believe that the anti-subsidy case is overwhelming and that tuition is an essential part of all desirable change in higher education. These views are exaggerated and create disturbances and bad faith, ultimately undermining reform.

A politics of realism, respect, and restraint is hardly tantamount to resignation. Consider the experiences with tax reform in several countries where a vicious cycle of obstruction and evasion has yielded some ground to a virtuous cycle of increased tax burdens, collection, political support, and active involvement by many individuals who had supported the old system (Berensztein 1995). Or consider the progress on tuition itself in a few countries. In Chile, the higher education system draws so heavily on tuition, sales, and contracts that it depends on the government for only one-third of its income. Costa Rica provides a more modest but promising example. Mexico has moved to a meaningful tuition in its state universities. This progress is easily overlooked, as international attention is riveted on repeated, unsuccessful attempts at reform, including the efforts at the national university in 1999.[6]

Advocates of change can applaud the skill and tact with which some reformers have broken through opposition. Seeds of change have been planted with measures such as fees for parking or examinations. An attractive approach is the visible and explicit application of fresh revenues to the improvement of student services. Another approach—which undermines claims that alternatives to subsidization are necessarily regressive—is the use of revenues to assist needy students. Yet another sound approach is to count increased cost recovery positively in formulas for whatever part of the public budget is tied to performance, as has been attempted in Bolivia. At a minimum, the government should assure institutions that more private income would not hurt their public income relative to their less reformist counterparts. It is essential to clarify repeatedly that advocacy of appropriately increased tuition is advocacy of a phased-in reform that must be tied to sound loan systems. And it is essential to clarify repeatedly that our support for increased tuition does not mean full financial responsibility on all or even most students. It does not mean full cost recovery for the higher education system.

Beyond tuition, other alternatives to public subsidization have gone further and in more countries (Schiefelbein 1996).[7] Colombia has long been an internationally heralded example of student loans for certain types of higher education. Like Brazil and unlike Chile, it allows loans for students at private institutions (Task Force 1994), although equity issues persist. Some public institutions have followed the lead of private ones in generating income through sales, services, and contracts. Most observers have insufficiently appreciated progress in this respect. A survey in Mexico showed that a great majority of institutions, facing restrictions in public subsidies, report at least some formal tie to business and many have special administrative units that generate funds through consulting and technical assistance (Casalet

---

[6] We could marvel at the irony of the rector of a state university (Nuevo León) supporting tuition at UNAM as a step toward standardization (homologación). The 1999 strike at UNAM is a sober reminder that sometimes even modest efforts at reform in funding can lead to disastrous disruption.

[7] This pattern of revenue diversification outpacing tuition is seen in Europe. Even in the United States, long the world leader in revenue diversity for public institutions, diversity has recently increased, as states have cut back. See Clark (1998).

and Casas 1998). UNICAMP (Brazil) generates significant income through the sale of services, but this revenue flows through separate foundations and stays outside the tracking system of the regular budget. Recently, the rector of Venezuela's national university could point proudly to the affiliated foundation that manages nine businesses and turns profits over to the university (Muñoz 1996). In short, we are witnessing the growth of some entrepreneurial enclaves inside public universities.

Diversification of funding involves public sources as well. Contracts, for example, come increasingly from government agencies as well as from private actors. The contracts supply important alternatives to basic subsidization from the education ministry's annual budget. In addition, government agencies competitively allocate special funds to productive professors, selective research projects, or institutional reform projects. Other alternative forms of financing are neither private nor public per se. Peru and some other countries have considered tax incentives to encourage individual and philanthropic giving.[8] Additionally, reform can attract international funds. The Inter-American Development Bank has supplied the most funds for higher education since the 1960s. In the 1990s it bolstered its financial commitment to higher education and other social sectors, while spelling out its emphasis on supporting reform. The World Bank has recently contributed to higher education in Argentina, Brazil, and Mexico. U.S. and European foundations and bilateral agencies do not loom as large as they did in the 1960s, but still serve as funding partners. Along with innovative international organizations, some universities have pioneered in creative swaps involving national debt and educational loans.

Tangible diversification of funding indicates progress. The view of Latin American higher education as simply funded through public subsidies becomes more and more mythical. Moreover, further diversification is now a major public policy issue. Even within public universities, advocates of diversification have increased in number, become more vocal, and are now less likely than before to be ostracized. Such progress, however uneven, is taking place in Argentina, Bolivia, Central America, and elsewhere.

---

[8] See Belaúnde and Marrou (1992). In Peru and elsewhere, the U.S.-based Americas Fund for Independent Universities and the National Endowment for Democracy have provided support for such efforts and tax incentives for donations.

Further Reform: Equity, Subsidization, and the Functions

All four functions of higher education need restructuring, but public policy must be sensitive to the very different nature and needs of each type of higher education. It must deal with a reality that continues to include substantial subsidization. The restructuring will be slower and more circuitous than advocates would like, partly because even an ideal future would see the protection of some subsidies and the bolstering of others.

Both the appropriate avenues for revenue diversification and the general criteria for public subsidization play out very differently according to the higher education function in question. The academic leadership function has the strongest claim to subsidization, but no function should be fully subsidized and none should be completely bypassed.

Academic Leadership Needs Major Subsidies

The public goods rationale for subsidization of high cost, high quality work applies to academic leadership more than to any other function in higher education. No country that wants significant research can expect students to pay for it. Worldwide, where higher education undertakes basic research and graduate education, it does so overwhelmingly in public institutions or with public subsidization of private ones. Not even the United States leaves the academic leadership function mostly to private markets.

Basic research must transcend the immediate market to gain the autonomy it needs, including some slack in its budgets. Private financing is not only inadequate; it also may come with strings that compromise institutional autonomy and academic freedom, thereby perverting the priorities essential to academic leadership. Higher education institutions should pursue more private financing, but with care to avoid unwarranted dependency on these sources or a loss of support and protection from public subsidization. Private financing must supplement, more than substitute for, public funds. Private funding can be a double-edged sword for the other functions as well, but professional development and technological training and development should respond to the market so that strings attached by private funders will be appropriate. The fact that private funding for general higher education usually means student contributions makes the specter of outside interference less ominous.

Although scientific fields offer the most widely accepted justifications for subsidies, the humanities also require attention because they tend to produce limited individual economic returns. As the rector of one national university points out, his challenge is not to find funding for contract-rich engineering, but for the humanities (Lavados 1996).[9] These concerns echo those of institutions in industrial countries that are increasingly subjected to restrictive public funding. Indeed, inadequate public funding of academically advanced higher education reflects a weak aspect in Chile's much-praised reforms, with deleterious consequences for libraries, laboratories, and research fields. The entrepreneurial university carries special risks for the funding and autonomy needs of academic leadership, but, ideally, the vigorous and creative generation of diverse and significant funds allows the university to cross-subsidize vital fields and endeavors that cannot go it alone in the marketplace (Clark 1998; James 1986). Insofar as public funds may also follow accountability criteria that are excessively restrictive for proper academic leadership, the university's ability to cross-subsidize can again be important.

Subsidies must reach individual students. In general, most students in question come from relatively privileged backgrounds and many have benefited from expensive private primary and secondary schools. However, future researchers require a long education and may not be well remunerated for their efforts and contributions; the creators of the public goods cited above usually attended academic leadership programs, including expensive graduate programs. Schools that are able to select promising youth and offer them the most exalted education play a major role in all industrial countries. They produce leaders by offering an education that usually only the very rich could afford if unsubsidized.

Thus, academic leadership requires generous funding, mostly public subsidization. The key to keeping the financial outlays under control, then, must be to avoid extending them to places where claims to this academic status are not sustained by performance.

---

[9] By contrast, the rectors at places such as the University of Costa Rica have found that certain areas of the humanities have done extremely well financially, for example, programs that offer English to native students or Spanish to foreign students.

Targeted Subsidies for Professional Development and Technological
Training and Development

By contrast, the professional development and technological training and development functions of higher education should receive financing partly through public subsidies and largely by the market—from tuition-paying students, contracts, and donations. The absence of market-generated income often indicates that this education is malfunctioning, which is not a good rationale for public subsidization. Governments should restrict public subsidies to targeted, justified conditions.

Professional development parallels academic leadership where it produces socially useful individuals as well as research that is not sufficiently rewarded by the private market. In this connection, public finance should not only compensate, it should provide incentives that attract more individuals to such jobs or to pledging at least part of their time for social service. For students who merely postpone financial rewards, loans are usually sufficient.

Much the same holds true for technological training and development. In general, technological training and development costs less than other higher education; therefore, the market, through loans, should make tuition a worthwhile investment for individual students, although public policy must also deal with the fact that students in technical programs tend to be from more modest backgrounds. Technological training and development includes expensive fields that yield substantial social payoffs, including some agricultural and high-end manufacturing training. In many fields, technological training and development contributes more to technology transfer than the value that salaries to graduates could possibly capture. Moreover, upgrading and productivity increases often require the assistance of skilled staff who are trained in the new technologies (soft and hard) and able to install, adapt, maintain, adjust, and repair new machinery and processes. These trained workers comprise the technological upgrading package. In addition, the technological training and development function includes research that sometimes deserves and even requires public funding. Thus, appreciating that there are vexing questions regarding the method and amount of public subsidies for technological training and development, we must recognize that there is a good case for some subsidization.

In sum, public subsidization is not only justified; professional development and technological training and development require it. What is not justified, but remains common, is public subsidization for the bulk of the training components of these functions.

Restructuring the Income Base for General Higher Education
General higher education may have the fewest clear-cut matches with the criteria for subsidization. This situation, coupled with its large size, makes overall cost recovery crucial.

General higher education exerts a relatively weak claim on the public purse. The public value in good general higher education and its contribution to a better-educated citizenry may be insufficient to place this type of education above other claims on public funds. In addition, much quasi-professional education in Latin America has dubious public value. In any case, the public sector should not subsidize general higher education at the expense of improvements in secondary education that could carry out the function as well or better.

Certainly no magic formula makes general higher education unworthy of public subsidization while making general secondary education worthy. Advanced societies increasingly enroll more than half the age cohort in higher education and offer greater opportunities for lifelong higher education. Eventually they may finance such undertakings more as they presently finance mass-based secondary education. A more pertinent point for the foreseeable future in Latin America is that general higher education by design can be comparatively inexpensive to subsidize. This may seem to cost-recovery hawks like unwarranted capitulation, but the public sector could achieve great cost savings by subsidizing this sort of higher education instead of mythical academic leadership or mythical professional development.

A persuasive case supports the argument for targeted subsidization aimed at helping Latin America's present quasi-professional education crack through structures and norms tied to professional forms, giving way to greater general higher education by design. This rationale supports subsidized reform projects, not ongoing subsidies to the bulk of general higher education. On balance, this book takes the position that the basic case for cost recovery applies to this general or quasi-professional portion of higher education. This formula for cost recovery may well leave some room for justifiable subsidization by legitimate political choice. However, we believe that the system of subsidies for higher education in Latin America needs major changes. Substantial restructuring of the private-public income mix for general higher education would come from greatly increasing the ratio of private to public funding. Reformed financial policy for general higher education in the public sector, greater growth in general higher education in the private sector, or both could change the ratio.

Incentives: Finance and Governance

Even if cost recovery accelerates, countries will continue to provide large subsidies to higher education. This conclusion rests on such factors as the strength of tradition and supportive political interests, the validity of certain arguments for subsidization, and the likelihood of further expansion of higher education. Given the large expenditures, officials must pay attention to the handling of funds. Because we focus on public policy and public subsidies, the discussion concerns mostly public higher education (although some matters of public policy and incentives for private higher education figure into the discussion on quality control).

A Vicious Cycle of Impunity

Major problems characterize the allocation and expenditures of public money worldwide, with severe manifestations in Latin America (Johnstone 1998; Salmi and Verspoor 1994; World Bank 1994). Here lies much of the explanation for inefficiency and inadequate performance. Any well-functioning higher education system needs sound governance with incentives for performance.[10] But Latin America is saddled with a system of subsidization that is intertwined with dysfunctional governance in an unhealthy cycle. The system suffers from too few rewards for socially useful behavior and too few penalties for antisocial actions. Governments as well as universities bear responsibility for this situation.

For the most part, governments allocate funds to public universities based on political bargaining and precedent or an overly simplistic input measure, such as number of students, or on a combination of

---

[10] This section deals with governance in terms of its close relationship with finance and incentives. It therefore says little about governance as a democratic process. However, the criticism of how certain types of participation have undermined sound incentives should not be construed as a general attack on democratic decisionmaking. Furthermore, a responsibly governed higher education system can contribute to a strong civil society, with ample forms of accountability, and an effective pluralist democracy (Levy 1999a).

the two methods (Brunner 1993). Such funding often translates into impunity for institutions. The system does not penalize institutions that perform poorly. Institutions do not penalize professors who show up unprepared for class or do not show up at all; the implicit bargain with students is that no work is done and no one complains. When reformers try to put things in order, strikes are common and the strikers pay no penalty. Those rectors who try to take a stand may pay the penalty of disruption or loss of position, while most rectors get along by passing the buck (literally). The flip side of this picture is equally bad. The system does not reward, or insufficiently rewards, institutions that perform well. The same situation holds true for units within institutions, administrators, professors, and students.

This is not a tale about a lack of modern management training. Management consultants or programs to train more professional administrators cannot immediately solve the governance problem. To put it more positively, management technique becomes critical once the political rules change enough to make its application rational.[11] And this is certainly not a tale about bad or dishonest people or about something that always happens. It is about a governance structure that commonly makes undesirable behavior rational and too infrequently offers incentives for desirable reform. Policymakers and the public should not blame the players; they should blame the rules and change them.

By international standards, Latin America's public universities have an unusual distribution of power. Clark (1983) coined the term "bottom-heavy" for institutions in Europe, referring to professorial power, usually the chaired professor. Moreover, a professorial role in governance makes more sense where the academic profession is truly advanced, with strong training, productivity, and accompanying norms (Altbach 1996; Clark 1987). Latin American bottom-heaviness, by contrast, refers more to student power, often alongside academically weak professors. At the extreme, as in Bolivia, Peru, and some Central

---

[11] The idea that training better managers is key to reforming governance problems is another myth. Similarly, finance is not a neutral, mechanical operation, but part of a politically determined incentive system. Where private finance operates better than public finance, it is not because it is apolitical, but because it is differently political. Moreover, sound incentives are compatible with public funding. For decades the United Kingdom's University Grants Committee rationally disbursed government funds to institutions. Plenty of room exists for Latin America's public universities to adapt some patterns of resource management more common in private universities and public and private research centers. This would help justify some degree of subsidization, whereas subsidization loses its validity when the subsidies are administered poorly.

American nations, higher education institutions have tripartite governance by students, professors, and administration officials (Instituto Universitario Ortega y Gasset 1998). Students' power has declined over the past twenty years, due to factors from both within and beyond the higher education system. Still, students remain powerful lobbyists against academic reform and changes that would tie finance more to performance (Brunner 1986; Levy 1991). Moreover, as student political power has diminished, unionization of the swelling ranks of faculty and other staff has raised new difficulties for rational matching of academic and economic incentives (Schwartzman 1998). Defenders laud co-government (co-gobierno) as democracy and erroneously equate it with institutional autonomy. However, it defies basic notions of democratic responsibility by giving so much power to groups that have little accountability to the funding public (Epstein 1974).

At the same time, the system often suffers from weaknesses among employers, states, and administrative hierarchies. Rectors may have strength through their coalitions with constituencies within their universities. They may have political strength, sometimes in antagonism to the government, sometimes based on the employment offered in the university's bloated bureaucracies (for example, in Northeast Brazil). But rectors rarely have the means of governance power that they need to promote institutional reform (Levy 1997).

Paradoxically, government has been too near to and too far from higher education. It has been too near in some cases by brutally repressing or crassly manipulating its public universities, or buying political support through existing politics, sometimes through political parties (Albornoz 1979). Government has been too far in other cases, in its lack of accountability for its expenditures and by the rarity of its partnership in major higher education reform.[12]

The unsatisfactory results of the common power configuration include the following.

- The higher education system suffers from excess conflict and insufficiently strong policies. The weak administrative and

---

[12] Comparisons come closer to the French than the Anglo-American pattern in two ways. First, the university is central to national politics. Second, the state is treated as a funder that should give the university what is needed, set some standardizing national legislation, and then maintain its distance. Notably, France and other European countries have disavowed this model (Neave 1988). For more on Latin American state-university relations in the 1980s, see Kovacs (1990); for the 1990s, see Kent (1996, 1997) and Courard (1993).

policymaking hierarchy cannot ensure a consistent, reliable vision or institutional profile.

- Students and faculty members use veto power, through formal representation or the credible threat of disruption, to block academically warranted reform. Their resistance results in debilitating bargains, weak decisions, and "nondecisions."
- Power struggles cause huge inefficiencies, including lost time.
- The system prohibits institutions from building or protecting nonpersonnel expenditures. For example, some rectors note that they could accomplish much more if only they could convert personnel savings into discretionary funds.

The term *homologación* sums up much of what is wrong. It highlights the myth that higher education can be dealt with largely as a single entity. *Homologación* refers to standard funding and other treatment regardless of performance. The rector of Venezuela's national university correctly labeled it an enemy of credibility and of policies based on productivity (Muñoz 1996). *Homologación* arises from political pressures within institutions and from lobbying efforts aimed at national legislation. For public institutions, it often ties state subsidies merely to enrollments, encouraging easy access and poor performance. For professors, excess job security and rewards tied to seniority lead to inadequate effort, retention of incompetent faculty members, and demoralization for those more inclined to perform well. Students face a similarly overly secure picture, with similar effects. The faulty incentive structure, not individuals with bad intentions, leads to behavior that is at odds with effective performance.[13]

Progress: Breaking the Cycle

Reformers have broken the cycle of impunity in many instances. Examples include cases that have gathered force over the years and recently launched initiatives. These precedents provide a substantial platform on which to build further positive links between incentives

---

[13] Subsidization that often goes beyond the absence of tuition to low-cost food, healthcare, and transportation exacerbates these effects. Youth who maintain their student status in such circumstances are less likely to be louts than rational people who are struggling (because they are ill prepared for university work or are engaged at an outside job for many hours per week). They likely hope somehow to manage their studies someday and could use the help in the meantime.

and governance. It is encouraging, too, that studies appear in individual countries that consider which ideas from abroad might be helpful regarding reform in the governance of public universities (see, for example, García de Fanelli 1998).

Leading private universities and research centers provide an established example of one response to the debilitating cycle in higher education. The relationship between choice and hierarchy is key. Students, teachers, and researchers who choose private institutions understand that they have to live by the rules. Often, they have chosen these institutions to escape the problems in public universities. The political dynamic in private institutions typically differs from the public sector. For example, rectors and directors at private institutions usually can speak with confidence in the name of their own institutions. They hold the power to deliver on their word without having to steer their proposals through a maze of potential veto points. They also tend to stay in office longer, at the pleasure of the boards that appoint them, without facing continual tests from mass-based voting constituencies.

Another important difference compared with the public university pattern lies in how income is obtained. Most private universities garner almost all their income from tuition and get only tax exemptions from the government (Levy 1986). This reliance on tuition promotes sounder internal management. Private institutions keep their personnel to a minimum to avoid raising costs over revenues. They respond to students as clients rather than as political lobbies. The number one problem with private institutions is the urge to offer substandard quality. In fact, the proportion of unacceptable levels of teaching and learning is staggering in some countries. These problems could be blamed on the fly-by-night operators or on the regulatory system that allows them to operate and grant legally valid diplomas. Private institutions should receive some mix of public regulation and contingent public funding. On the positive side, some private institutions offer some respectable alternatives to the cycle that is characteristic of institutions in the public sector.

Research centers (public, private, and those within universities) often map the future in terms of obtaining resources that are linked to performance. These institutions of choice run with internal hierarchies and resolve, depend on competitive funding (both private and public), and offer little job security. Ties to markets, peer review, and evaluation are more prevalent than in other higher education institutions.

Indeed, the research centers are often the ports of entry for these industrial country norms because they are appropriately required for international assistance.[14]

These innovations originate and flourish largely outside the realm of grand public policy. But, as box 5.1 describes, Brazil implemented significant reform at the graduate level through major changes in national policy, although it accomplished a lot by bypassing the education ministry (Durham and Schwartzman 1992).

The region has experienced an increase in national policies aimed at breaking the cycle of impunity for universities. The new contract, described by Brunner (1993), is similar to Europe's new evaluative state, described by Neave (1988). Under the new contract, the receipt of public money depends more on performance that is accountable to public goals.[15] This change follows the logic of philanthropic giving; it aims strategic, targeted sums at reform and at leveraging that reform for effects on the broader system.[16]

Chile is once more the lead case. Democratic policymakers did not overturn the previous (military) government's move toward decreasing the public share of total expenditures, combined with greater performance-based funding of the remaining public share (Brunner 1990). A formula that has gained considerable praise gives extra money to institutions on the basis of the percentage of top secondary school graduates they attract, as measured by aptitude tests administered to the graduates.[17]

---

[14] The success of these centers pertains largely to the academic leadership function; in applied research and training, it also applies to the technological training and professional development functions. In fact, the linkage between performance and finance could easily be too tight for much of academic research and graduate education, with too much accountability tied to immediately tangible performance and, therefore, too little academic autonomy (Levy 1996a).

[15] New policy should not be fundamentally about tightly conditioned annual subsidies for institutions. Along with some conditional funding, there could be increased noninvasive formula budgeting where budgets have to date been based heavily on precedent, politics, or overly simple formulas (for example, by numbers not weighted by field of study).

[16] A welcome corollary is that, as recipients see less automatic money from government and as they perceive some autonomy lost by following government's new criteria too closely, they have increased incentives to seek alternative financing.

[17] To the extent these tests aim at getting extra resources to the academically most able, and to the extent they reward and stimulate healthy competition, the innovation is sound. But aptitude testing is a tool very much linked to conventional academic quality rather than to value added. It is largely irrelevant to competition among and improvement within the overwhelming majority of institutions and the functions they perform.

Box 5.1. Incentives for Graduate Programs and Research: Brazil Leads the Way

Brazil's graduate programs and research largely escape perverse budget patterns (Castro 1989). Special agencies (CAPES, CNPQ, FINEP, and FAPESP) play a major role, staffed by experts and drawing on peer reviews for graduate scholarships and research. The agencies offer a wide menu of options: grants on a project by project basis according to the intrinsic merits of proposals, rewards for outstanding programs, salary supplements for researchers (as at the French CNRS), and discretionary funds for the best graduate schools. In addition, many graduate schools contract to provide services and research and development to private and public agencies.

In sum, the graduate system is driven more by competitive funds, on which so many researchers directly depend, than by fixed university budgets. And so it operates in a different league compared with the undergraduate programs at the same universities.

Other national experiences have varied. The Mexican reforms cited early in the book were induced in large part by the government's new financial policy. Fund for the Improvement of Higher Education (FOMES) is a special fund targeted for reform. Although small in absolute terms, FOMES funds have helped change the rational cost/benefit ratio for several rectors; they learn to manage resources in terms of performance once they see more gains in modernizing than in populist policies (Ornelas 1996; Kent 1998).

A similar story unfolds in Argentina. Its Fondo de Mejoramiento de la Calidad Universitaria (FOMEC) has received more consistently good grades for its judgment, integrity, and assistance (Brunner and Martínez Nogueira 1999). It has done much to stimulate the idea that public universities ready to launch reforms aimed at improved performance deserve more than counterparts that fail to act. It has stimulated healthy competition and has encouraged institutions to strengthen their ability to prioritize, to gather and utilize data, and to manage themselves. FOMEC has also stimulated the generation and sharing of resources. FOMEC complements legislation that moves away from *homologación*. At the same time, the University of Buenos Aires has developed some funding sources tied to performance or to the productive sector (Mollis 1995).

By contrast, Venezuela has enacted legislation that moves the country toward *homologación*. Bolivia has not delivered resources according to the incentive-based contracts it developed a few years ago (Contreras 1996; Urquiola 1993). The country's reform efforts still face a cloudy future.

In the absence of systemic reform, several institutions have gained increased ability to reform. Although Brazil's national legislative attempts to revamp the incentive structure at the undergraduate level have been frustrated by forceful interest groups, changes in the incentive structure at the local level have produced encouraging changes. Magalhães Castro (1995) finds that better rules make a difference. Efficiency in the allocation of funding improved greatly when São Paulo's state universities started receiving lump-sum budgets in place of those delivered by restrictive categories. For example, given control over budgetary decisions, department heads cut excess personnel and applied the money to more productive ends.

Incentives for professors are much more widespread than a revamping of state funding for institutions. A good example is Mexico's National System of Researchers, which provides funding for about 6,000 positions on a (mostly) merit, peer-judged basis. Most state universities still have basic *homologación* and union pressure to maintain it; however, awards for full-time faculty members now extend to teaching as well as research professors (Ornelas 1996). Argentina has made available financing for fellowships, institutes, research programs, and professors of graduate study, without extending those benefits across the board to all professors. Like Venezuela, probably most countries now have some merit-based funds available regardless of "university" or private-public status.

Insidious relationships between financial incentives and governance remain widespread, but it would be a serious error to ignore the substantial breaks in the cycle. Instead, we applaud these breaks and encourage more and deeper ones.

Further Reform: How Incentives and Functions Should Match

Further reforms must aim at governing different types of higher education so that they respond more naturally to incentives and disincentives. The academic leadership function in particular requires careful discrimination in the incentives and governance employed. Because this is the function that has the greatest justification for public funding and autonomy, it is here that public policy can best remain true to a now much-denounced notion: steady, generous funding without demand for direct, easily measurable accountability to either the government or the job market. Two caveats bear repetition. First, public policy must save money by according less, not more, such treatment to places whose academic aspirations far outstrip their achievements. Second, there must be plenty of competitive (market) mechanisms within the academic world, for example, to attract the best graduate students and faculty, as well as extra money.

Funding for the other functions depends on making sure that annual government subsidies no longer constitute nearly all the income for public institutions. Reducing the share of subsidies in total income will reduce the need to condition it tightly because the trust or autonomy granted will cost less. At the same time, it must be clear that the money works for the particular purposes that justify its disbursement (for example, technology transfer or service to the poor). Any public funds going to what is presently quasi-professional education should be accompanied by mechanisms that guard against squandering.

For the professional development and technological training and development functions, the influential roles of practitioners and employers are crucial to getting the incentives right. Notwithstanding the important circumstances that yield contrary indications, professional and technological training require less autonomy from the marketplace and more accountability to it.

But here again, generalizations should yield to discrimination by function. Many observers say that higher education in Latin America should become more tied to business and industry. We present ideas for achieving that, but we also emphasize where there should not be close ties. General higher education would appear to have the least direct role, although some units could include sound business orientations. The academic leadership function would come into play partly by educating some students who turn out to be business people and also through joint research enterprises. However, neither academic leadership nor general higher education would have the degree of ties regarding curriculum and representation on boards that we outlined for professional development and technological training and development.

Most conversations and policies regarding governance are too generalized. They refer to government rather than to the panoply of pertinent external actors. Accountability and autonomy should depend on the function. While calls for decreased state control and increased institutional autonomy are appealing and often appropriate, their generality is dangerous and creates new policy myths (World Bank 1994; Neave and van Vught 1994; Maassen and van Vught 1994). Regarding planning, comprehensive efforts aimed at the "best policy" for the system can be the worst sort of planning.[18]

The radical restructuring of governance requires not one but several formulas. All reform formulas must include a common element of an incentive structure that stimulates improved performance.

Tools for Quality Control

Evaluation is crucial to the reform of incentives. Evaluation, including various sorts of accreditation, is a topic of great interest in higher education in Latin America, as it is in most of the world.[19] It is a keystone in the rising concern to improve quality.

Paltry Evaluation in the Face of Inadequate Policy

We believe that the average quality of higher education in Latin America is low and decreasing. Up until about 30 years ago, dubious growth remained much more common in the public sector. More recently, many nations—including Brazil, Chile, Colombia, Costa Rica, the Dominican Republic, and El Salvador—have allowed the creation of mass demand-absorbing private institutions of higher education. Concern over egregiously low quality is warranted for both sectors.

Because quality is far from uniformly low and depends very much on our views of what ought to be accomplished, evaluation must be attuned to the different forms of higher education. A bad but common mistake is to evaluate one form of education for what it is not or what it cannot be. Some critics blame quasi-professional schools for

---

[18] Discriminating central planning that is sensitive to the different higher education realities can be quite positive. Further, if institutions can develop governance structures more adequate to their own internal mix of functions and performance, then a great increase in institutional planning would be a priority. Certainly, neither governments nor any external agency should even try to micromanage institutions.

[19] See, for example, Neave (1988) on Europe, Vessuri (1993) on Latin America, and Malo and Velázquez (1998) on Mexico.

not preparing students for the profession indicated on their diplomas. But these critics fail to perceive that the students may be getting a serious education, which could help them in whatever they subsequently do. Engineering schools may be considered excellent because their teachers publish a lot even though the quality of teaching is deplorable and graduates are inadequately prepared to face the labor market.

In some cases, evening students who work full time perform as well as full-time students at expensive public universities. Few observers laud the evening students for their respectable results, although many deprecate the students from the big-name university for their mediocre performance. Most evaluation efforts, certainly most official efforts, have not succeeded in targeting the real function performed by the institution or school. This problem has contributed to excessive trashing of what is not professional or academic leadership, and to controls based on unrealistic requirements.[20] In short, it contributes to rampant confusion and distortions. It also makes for poor precedent for contemporary reform.

Latin America has been left with too little effective evaluation. In fact, it has too little of virtually every healthy kind of evaluation. It needs more evaluations that are not part of any formal accreditation system. It would also do well to have more official evaluation, if handled well. This might include a consensual, legalized notion of what all higher education should be—as long as any such listing is kept to a minimum. It might even include composite comparisons (comparing institutions as opposed to just comparing an aspect, unit, or function among institutions) of institutions as a means to getting the incentives right—as long as great care is taken to compare similar functions, and to do so with reserve and flexibility (for example, allowing for explanatory responses from evaluated places).

The higher education system desperately needs evaluations that lead to building, gathering, and disseminating information to help all parties act more rationally in increasingly competitive markets. Students and employers need information to overcome their problems of accurate identification. Professors need information so they can work

---

[20] For example, measures to control quality wind up protecting "university" graduates, and licenses are required where there is no objective need for them. In Brazil, the requirement that prospective schools prove a market exists for their graduates leads to corruption.

in the best institutions for their skills. And governments need information to move away from standardized funding and toward a more discriminating policy of funding different functions in different ways, depending on performance.

Almost everyone agrees from the outset that higher education needs more evaluation. There is no consensus, however, on what information to gather or how to use it. Evaluation that generates accurate information for all parties concerned is almost always good. Evaluation that creates healthy competition among schools and students is likewise desirable. The same can be said for evaluation that triggers administrative and legal action in case results do not reach a threshold of quality. It is up to the state to monitor its own schools and to prevent abuse on the part of unscrupulous or incompetent private operators. Licensing practices in cases of areas involving safety is also a common and totally acceptable use for evaluation.

Unfortunately, many places use accreditation to create market reserves for graduates with the "right" diplomas. Formal mechanisms of evaluation control access to occupations. An overgeneralized carryover from the medieval guild system, where access to occupations was controlled by law or custom, is one of the infirmities of higher education in Latin America. As a result, accreditation becomes a highly politicized battleground to create market reserves for those who have negotiated the legal and bureaucratic hurdles to obtain the authorization to issue diplomas. The public universities lobby to prevent the private institutions from competing in the same market. Already accredited private operators support the public operators' anti-competitive lobbying. Corruption sets in and the quality of instruction becomes a lesser preoccupation.

Progress: Building on Existing Evaluation and Accreditation

Notwithstanding the general lack of sound evaluation, there is precedent to build upon. This precedent includes a combination of long-standing practice and recent initiatives.

A Heritage of Evaluation

Where higher education has worked reasonably well, evaluation has already been at play. It often eludes analysis because it is nonofficial. Well-prepared students and professors make some assessment of institutions and programs before choosing where to go. Many employers and clients have been able to hire professionals based on some rational assessment. The open announcement of job openings and competitions (concurso) for hiring professors or for defense and promotion after initial hiring is a formal and traditional practice.

Foreign agencies have initiated more official evaluation programs. Through evaluation of potential and projects, they have planted the seeds for an evaluation culture (Schwartzman 1991; Levy 1996a). Some private and public research centers have achieved further development of this culture, such as Chile's CIEPLAN and Venezuela's IVIC (Vessuri 1997). The culture also has gained a place in national councils of science and technology and other public agencies that deliver discretionary funds to eligible individuals, graduate programs, and research projects. Brazil has leapt way ahead of the rest of the region with its councils and accreditation for graduate education. Brazil's system distinguishes real from false academic leadership programs. It shows how much can be accomplished through the sensible use of data. The Commission for Training of Higher Education Personnel (CAPES) uses quantitative data to complement peer reviews. It visits the graduate programs and ranks them; it is not uncommon to find the program grades posted at the entrance of the administrative offices (Castro 1989).

Two other common and spreading sites of progress operate below the system level and provide precedents for formal accreditation. First, traditional professions (for example, medicine and engineering) and some newer or less prestigious professions (for example, journalism) have sometimes developed their own accreditation systems. Second, prestigious private universities have sought accreditation through foreign associations, including in the United States. Examples include the Universidad de Los Andes and the Universidad Javeriana in Colombia and several institutions in Mexico. Like some Bolivian counterparts, these examples show private institutions supporting or even pushing the creation of a national accreditation system.[21]

---

[21] Private institutions can also indirectly, through competition, stimulate the development of accreditation by reaching outside national boundaries. This has been common in Greece and several countries in Asia and Central and Eastern Europe, where private higher education that is denied full legal recognition gains legitimacy through foreign ties and through foreign or private domestic employment markets (Patrinos 1995; Breslin 1999). Over time, public institutions may need to gain such legitimacy.

The Advent of National Accreditation Systems

National accreditation systems add to the evaluation landscape, which has abundant precedents for the licensing of new institutions.[22] Throughout the region, the idea of a national accreditation system for ongoing as well as initial assessment is under consideration. In fact, acceptance of the general idea is suddenly widespread, notwithstanding the great differences that persist over what that system should look like. Bolivia and several countries in Central America have initiated capacity building. Argentina has a formal national accreditation system. Mexico has created separate accrediting mechanisms and subsystems for science and technology, graduate education, and higher education institutions in general, although implementation has often been superficial, begrudging, and formalistic.

Chile and Colombia provide two leading national cases of progress, despite problems and unanticipated results. Ayarza (1995) outlines the main system in Chile, which is run by a public autonomous national council, with its own funds and with members selected by the higher education institutions. The council was created over concern about the unmonitored quality of the booming private sector, to protect users and provide a public guarantee of some minimum level; new private institutions are now subject to review for their first six to eleven years. Competitively selected peers evaluate institutions based on a guidebook with twelve criteria. These touch on matters such as curriculum, academic personnel, and libraries, although it is unclear what constitutes grounds for a high rating. The science and technology council runs a second Chilean system. It is less autonomous but is voluntary, required only of places that compete for that council's funds. The vagueness of criteria and subjectivity of judgments are criticized, yet the alternative used in the first system runs the risk that specific objective criteria are insensitive to the value added outside academic leadership functioning. Finally, dissatisfaction with this second council has led to a third system; voluntary, autonomous, and run by the council of rectors, this system accredits programs rather than institutions.

Colombia implemented its system following study, design, and public seminars. The creators of Colombia's accreditation system in-

---

[22] That licensing was often pro forma in Mexico. It had restrictive periods in Brazil in the 1970s. Temporary restrictions have been especially common for new private institutions in Peru and Argentina.

cluded several positive features: distinction among university, technological, and narrower technical programs; links between accreditation
by professional program and accreditation by institution; space for
self-study, peer review, and evaluation based on the institution's goals;
a national commission composed of esteemed academic figures and
with academic autonomy from government, but with practical political ties to government authority; and emphasis on spreading information to the public (Orozco 1994).

Maximum Progress through Limited Accreditation Systems
Colombia and Chile have included many of the better features of a
national accreditation system and have avoided the worst of the overly
generalized features often proposed. The region would progress by
emulating their example. Nonetheless, the pioneering efforts provide
lessons for identifying and limiting some dangerous tendencies.

The main caution is to avoid an accreditation system that seeks
to apply one ample set of criteria to the whole system. Only modestly
better is the development of just two sets of criteria for universities
and technical institutes. Handling diverse activities with overly similar
mechanisms is an old mistake repeated in the new form of accreditation. Leading international advocates of increased evaluation report
that countries risk lowering quality where they overzealously establish
national standards (Kells 1992; Moodie 1986).

The typical set of systemwide accreditation criteria relies on conventionally defined academic quality. Thus, it misjudges three of the
four functions. It ignores the fact that institutions with lower conventional academic quality may have higher net quality or a different mix
of quality. It produces meaningless, stigmatizing, or misleading conclusions. For example, it would find the University of Chile to have higher
quality than Chile's professional institutes, which, in turn, would have
higher quality than the technical training centers. Where rewards at-
tach to higher scores, such a system contributes to the pernicious incentives to pursue officially favored directions when others could be
better done; it also discourages meaningful self-study and dissemina-
tion of honest information. Some public university rectors have sug-
gested that the IDB should choose the best ten Latin American
universities as models by which to judge and promote the quality of
the region's higher education. This sort of proposal fundamentally misses
the point, as do most references to pursuing the highest level of quality. If such phrases contained multiple meanings of quality, they could

be unobjectionable, but the inclination is to define quality as an objective thing, identifiable and measurable.[23]

In addition to their other dangers, overly ambitious proposals risk falsely inflating expectations. The myth that higher education does not require external evaluation yields to the myth that a single broadly conceived external evaluation system can almost instantly bring a surge in quality. When such expectations are dashed, opportunities for more reasonable change may also wane.

Europe's initial experiences are instructive. Like Latin America, Europe has seen the need for more evaluation and explicit attention aimed at improving quality. This is a retreat from faith in professional autonomy and in a priori national rules followed by minimal inspection with no a posteriori evaluation. That was essentially the Continental model, largely emulated in Latin America—but with less national standardization and more institutional autonomy, sometimes to the point where there was barely a requirement to *rendir cuentas,* or show that money given was spent for declared purposes (Levy 1994). So Europe launched national evaluation systems with great expectations (Neave and van Vught 1991). Generalizing across nations, analysts report positive results regarding efficiency in resource management, but little regarding ability to measure quality, let alone to justify the idea that this evaluation would lead to much higher quality. "Infatuation" and vigor have turned to disenchantment and stagnation as the process proves costly, unable to assess numbers in context, politicized, and irrelevant to value added. Interestingly, though, efforts oriented to particular functions and institutions have worked better than those aimed at national standards (Jongbloed and Westerheijden 1994:47–48).

Caution does not justify policy inaction. Higher education in Latin America needs greater evaluation in more rational cycles of perfor-

---

[23] While acknowledging that component parts and measures are complex and difficult to quantify, many still think they can be added together into one common, composite, comparable score. A favorite analogy is that quality is like beauty: we struggle to define it precisely but we know it when we see it. The analogy is perfect because it is perfectly wrong, wrong in parallel fashion for beauty and quality. Neither is an objective concept. Identification of a concept with some particular view or taste has prejudicial and debilitating consequences for those who do not fit. This hardly means that all higher education has equal quality, or that all definitions have equal validity or are without any objective content; it means that no one definition should be promulgated and then put into operation by an official national body (Levy 1996b).

mance-evaluation-improved performance. Denial of a national system that ranks institutions on a common official definition of quality leaves room for prudent national systems. More importantly, it leaves room for multiple evaluations, formal and informal, as multiple actors use their own definitions of good quality, based on their own values and interests. The case against one centralized evaluation system is not a case for avoiding evaluation; it is a case for many evaluations.

Further Reform: Four Functions, Four Formulas for Improvement

Efforts to evaluate the different types of higher education should center on the distinctions among each of its four functions. Accreditation and other forms of evaluation should provide information on the real functions performed in institutions and units within them. This information would help to explode the myths about what higher education does. It could also serve as a major step in matching functions to incentives and governance. By focusing on real functions and rewarding institutions that perform well, a sound educational system would reduce the tendency to mislabel undertakings or to pursue unreachable ones. It is better to be judged by a general education or technological function done moderately well than by an academic leadership or professional function done sparsely or poorly. Analysis by function indicates that authorities can appropriately effect evaluation largely through a system of institutional accreditation for only one of the four functions, general higher education. Alternative forms of evaluation are more natural and appropriate for the other three functions, although institutional accreditation may have a role for them as well.

Academic Leadership

Accreditation is not fundamental to the academic leadership function. Indeed, imposed criteria can undercut the autonomy and academic freedom needed for exploration and excellence. But nonintrusive accreditation can help, while not hurting, the evaluation system, as in the case of the Ivy League schools and leading public universities in the United States. With nonintrusive accreditation, the standards consist of almost completely unthreatening minimums and conventional measures of academic quality. The accreditation process provides an occasion for self-study and feedback from peer review and it provides information to pertinent external actors. The key is that any accreditation should complement, not undermine, the evaluations fundamental to the scholarly world.[24]

Professional Development
Accreditation should complement the mostly market-oriented evaluations fundamental to the professional development function. An overly general national accreditation system runs the danger of imposing academic leadership criteria, such as the ratio of full-time to part-time professors. In addition, Latin American higher education should not strive for a U.S.-style institutional accreditation system. In Latin America, universities often consist of loose collections of professional or quasi-professional programs. It makes little sense for the accreditation process to focus on institutions that lack academic and administrative coherence.

The most appropriate accreditation for the professional development function applies to the level of the professional program rather than the institution. Any institutional accreditation must be flexible and limited enough to allow for specific and demanding professional accreditation (perhaps at the program level). In the United States, only dismal institutions fail to get institutional accreditation, but many professional development programs cannot meet the accrediting standards of their professional associations. Professional accreditation has precedent in Latin America, too, and offers hope for identifying the quasi-professional programs that probably should be reoriented as general higher education. Voluntary and private professional accrediting agencies can draw on the profession itself for criteria and evaluators.

Technological Training and Development
The technological training and development function may be the one least appropriate for accreditation. It might apply to the private providers operating in the areas of inexpensive and generic skills, such as secretarial training, bookkeeping, and computing, which can suffer from recurrent fraud and incompetence. But the job market provides the basic mechanism for monitoring and promoting quality in technological training and development. The government plays a role by promoting the flow of accurate information. At the same time, public

---

[24] At institutions that are motivated by internal norms, tying funding to invidious evaluation can hurt delicate group dynamics, professional sensibilities, risk-taking, and ultimately performance (Kohn 1994).

technical institutes should come under direct government control where appropriate.

Accreditation of technological training and development schools partly parallels accreditation of professional development schools. However, the fast-paced changes in the job market probably express needs better and accreditation runs the risk of fixing constraints that inhibit swift flexibility. As with the professional development function, accreditation could play a selective role where programs claim to go beyond training to research or extension.

General Higher Education
The greatest need for institutional accreditation lies in general higher education, both for the quasi-professional portion that is dubious and for the most valuable general higher education.

This function especially requires accreditation because it suffers from low quality, confusion, and meager alternative means of evaluation. The market is too slow, tangential, and indirect; conventional academic norms are both too demanding and too skewed to activities outside the core of pertinent teaching. Here is where the need for information is keenest and its provision scantiest. Students and employers need information to identify the quality of institutions and to identify frauds. Government needs to know which institutions deserve annual subsidies, assuming it chooses to retain some funding for this function. It needs to be able to identify which institutions perform well enough to justify public aid to students. And it needs information to identify which institutions should be closed.

Consistent with the general cautions about overly ambitious national accreditation systems, three considerations should be paramount in designing accreditation for general higher education. First, the need for information must be tempered by the nebulous nature of the measurement, especially because the evaluation of teaching is generally less developed than the evaluation of research.[25] Second, the authorities

---

[25] Neither direct job placement nor conventional gauges of academic quality fit neatly, although they can be part of the assessment of general higher education. Some proponents of ambitious accreditation systems fall back on the concept of relevance without defining it or acknowledging different, legitimate views of what is worthwhile relevance. What really matters is getting a good education through whatever credible area or method. Perhaps the most suitable kind of testing would be something akin to the rage in contemporary U.S. evaluations for accountability: assessment of student development in such matters as intellectual growth. But the technology for such testing remains crude.

should avoid making accreditation too threatening. Of course, some level of threat may provide an incentive to reform and any worthwhile accreditation must foster the desire to improve. However, there is understandable trepidation connected with the provision of sorely needed accurate information and institutions are potentially vulnerable. A system with tough consequences could provide major incentives for institutions to distort the data or otherwise not cooperate. Such cautionary thoughts may favor accreditation systems that have a dichotomous bottom line approval or disapproval (tempered perhaps with space for probation), with a very modest threshold for approval.

A third caution in developing accreditation for general higher education is that, like almost all evaluation, it should be sensitive to private-public dimensions, particularly as regards subsidization. Much of the clamoring for institutional accreditation has concerned the new private institutions that are largely quasi-professional and have incentives to offer low quality with poor teaching.[26] But the fact that these institutions almost never get public funding reduces the rationale for subjecting them to a national accreditation system, although the justification for public regulation to protect the public trust remains. The justification for accreditation is more compelling for public institutions that absorb subsidies and tend to be less controlled by the need to attract paying students. By the same token, private institutions would be included alongside public ones where they are allowed to solicit public funding.[27]

To sum up, the report card on evaluation is worrying but neither totally negative nor hopeless. It is plagued by too little effort and by problems with past and present efforts. But a combination of healthy, growing precedents and additional criteria that are sensitive to real functions can light a path to improved performance.

---

[26] The many examples include private institutions in Costa Rica and the Dominican Republic. Brazil in the 1970s was probably the first major example. Formally nonprofit institutions, they have some incentive to overinvest in real estate or infrastructure that they do not use well educationally. The room for such "cheating" comes from the imperfect markets that include inadequate information for students and employers, as well as legal provisions that guarantee jobs for degree holders (Castro and Navarro 1999).

[27] This could include private institutions engaged in academic leadership. Openness to private higher education would also include professional programs seeking the credibility that would help them compete for students and jobs. If that puts competitive pressure on comparable public programs, so much the better. Accreditation should also be open, indeed required, for private institutions seeking to gain or maintain the privilege that their degrees carry an automatic legal right to practice a profession—although that is a privilege that should be decreased for both private and public education.

CHAPTER 6

BETWEEN STATUS QUO AND NEOLIBERAL EXTREMES

The critical analysis of higher education in Latin America and suggestions for policy reform may lead some to tag this book as a hostile document and lump it indiscriminately with mounting attacks directed at the region's public universities. Such dismissiveness, whether as honest conviction or as political strategy, is a common reaction of those who defend the status quo. We seek in this conclusion to combat that dismissiveness. But we also seek to identify common ground with many in higher education and elsewhere who truly want reform, yet regard prominent critiques of Latin American higher education as ill-conceived. It is thus crucial to distinguish our critique and our proposals from what is often loosely labeled a neoliberal approach. Drawing this distinction provides a way to summarize and synthesize the main points of the preceding chapters without merely repeating them.

How much our points do or do not fit neoliberalism depends on how neoliberalism is defined. In fact, it is usually not defined, but rather attacked or advanced in an ad hoc fashion, often with reference to some particular or presumed aspect of it. However much this observation holds for neoliberalism generally, it certainly holds internationally for neoliberalism in higher education policy. In discussions about higher education, critics use the term neoliberal more than avowed supporters, so that the term usually carries a negative connotation.[1] Here we want to distinguish our critique and our proposals from what is often loosely labeled a neoliberal approach.

Notwithstanding the vagueness and variability of the term "neoliberal," the neoliberal assessment of higher education comprises

---

[1] Perhaps the best known or most important single document that is widely called neoliberal is the World Bank's *Lessons from Experience* (1994). For a prominent, ranging critique of the World Bank's policy agenda, see Buchert and King (1995). Although many of our points are at odds with the World Bank's, many of its positions do not conform to any neoliberal stereotype.

certain key elements. It denounces the status quo. It ignores or mini-mizes reform efforts to date and characterizes performance as poor, inefficient, noncompetitive, inequitable, and lacking in accountability. It finds only limited or misdirected links to the market and the economy. It claims that the system has grown and continues to grow too easily and that public costs are excessive. It says that economically and aca-demically perverse political and social factors drive the system.

According to the neoliberal approach, the system requires fun-damental reform. The core of the proposed reform is financial. It would end automatic reliance on public subsidies and tie remaining subsidies to performance. It strives to attack the problems and develop a more productive, efficient system. Reform would involve the introduction or expansion of private financing, cost recovery at public institutions, growth in private higher education, and other low-cost alternatives to traditional public university education.

Our analysis makes most of these points and, to some extent, could be labeled neoliberal. But if the story stops there, it stops pre-maturely. Often we have found some truth in a neoliberal charge or proposal, yet not enough to credit it as a decent generalization or a viable policy that should be pursued regardless of others' views or the political cost. In many cases, we find the actual experience more trou-bling than the positive myths about higher education. However, in contrast to the neoliberal perspective, we also find more positive and varied performance than indicated by the negative myths propagated by many of higher education's critics. Some of our proposals overlap neoliberal proposals and others contradict them. Much of what we have written shows where common neoliberal points do not apply, where they apply only in certain ways or under certain conditions, or how they apply only weakly or in ways unlike the way commonly depicted by zealous neoliberals. What we have written is therefore quite different from what is often depicted as neoliberalism. The dif-ference arises partly from real differences between our approaches and neoliberals' common ones and partly from exaggerated differ-ences where critics stereotypically portray neoliberalism.

In contrast with the neoliberal approach, we emphasize the broad role of higher education in national development. Higher education has vital tasks—cultural, social, political, philosophical, and quintessentially academic—that go beyond immediate economic ser-vice. Higher education has research and service functions that go be-yond teaching and certainly beyond mere training. Higher education cannot be wholly subordinated to any easy or narrow measure of what it does, let alone what it should do.

We note the positive accomplishments of higher education in Latin America and its relevance for wider national development. Higher education fits into the economy as well as social and political life in certain substantial ways. Some higher education institutions and many units within institutions have made impressive contributions and progress. Growth has brought much that is desirable, as well as problems. Higher education has diversified in multifaceted ways—across socioeconomic classes, institutions, sectors, and programs of study.

We reject the portrayal of higher education in Latin America as unchanging. Historically and recently, it has achieved reforms, some through large-scale public policy, others through a variety of uncoordinated initiatives. Because there are continued achievements and changes, we cannot endorse a *borrón y cuenta nueva* approach, scrapping all and starting from scratch.

Whereas neoliberalism often comes across as ahistorical, we trace how the evolution of new functions and institutions contributes to today's underappreciated complexity. Although neoliberals may favor the diversification of institutions and tasks, their analyses are usually insufficiently sensitive to diversity. Even where it has something important to say about contemporary practice or reform, neoliberalism tends to overgeneralize. For example, it advocates privatization, whether through change within public institutions or through the growth of private ones. We agree that many benefits can come from privatization, but we also note the dangers and trade-offs. Neoliberalism is not alone in promoting overly general diagnoses and remedies; our point here is that it does not escape that tendency.

The four-part typology of functions plays a central role in our analysis. It is likely that some of the distinctions that emerge would be embraced or accommodated by many neoliberals. However, neoliberalism has not recognized or at least identified most of these distinctions. Instead, neoliberalism explicitly prescribes systemwide reforms, without consideration of points of applicability.

We are very supportive of the true academic leadership function and praise its growth. Indeed, here we are pointedly pro-growth. We consider ourselves anti-neoliberal in identifying its principal needs: high expenditures, overwhelmingly public funding, protection from most direct accountability to taxpayers or governmental measures of efficiency or equity, and great autonomy from most external economic market pressures. Our analysis and prescriptions also clash starkly with broad neoliberal tenets on what we call general higher education. We emphasize that positive results can bring growth in both economic and non-economic terms when more and more citizens can think critically and we again look for substantial autonomy from the market. At the same time, we share concern over unwarranted expansion, especially when publicly funded, and advocate regulation through accreditation.

Our agenda comes closer to the neoliberal perspective with regard to the professional development and technological training and development functions of higher education. We emphasize the market's signals, financing, and controls. However, we stress elements of each function that transcend the market. We emphasize a pro-growth stance regarding technological training and development. And we argue for protection of professional development, which Latin America has often performed admirably, albeit alongside surging quasi-professional education.

Similarly, when we come to consider particular policy concerns, we mix endorsement of certain neoliberal positions with qualification or rejection of others. We agree that public subsidization constitutes an excessive share of the present higher education dollar. Subsidization often favors those who do not need it as much as others. Much of it goes to favor people and institutions that do not perform adequately. Thus, present subsidization is both inefficient and inequitable.

Nonetheless, various forms of lower-cost alternatives to public universities are growing. Two-fifths of enrollments are in the private sector, which usually receives little or no public subsidization. Public institutions have made notable progress in attracting nontraditional revenues. Moreover, the neoliberal portrayal of an equity crisis is exaggerated. We do not favor a general policy of having students pay full cost; instead, we favor movement toward having more students pay what they can afford to pay with loans.

Regarding the nexus between finance and governance, we agree with the neoliberal point that government inappropriately or indiscriminately gives subsidies. We have explained how and why the incentive structure gives different actors too much or too little power. Norms like *homologación* cripple competition and desirable policy change. However, the private sector often breaks from these patterns. In addition, some public institutions have reformed, whether on their own initiative or in response to revamped national policies.

Many countries have special, performance-based funds for research, teaching, or institutional improvement. We call for expansion of such competitive funding. How and where that expansion should take place depends on the function. We suggest how each function requires a different mix of incentives. And we spell out how each function requires a different governance structure, with different roles for the government, the market, and a range of higher education actors. We therefore reject reforms, neoliberal as well as others, that are essentially one-size-fits-all.

Regarding quality control, we argue that average performance is seriously deficient. Efforts at improvement must include information and evaluation. But we also have identified and lauded evidence of estimable performance, and not just in pockets of academic leadership. Moreover, our identification of what works decently guides many of our recommendations for improvement.

Even where we call for radical changes, we discriminate by function, as neoliberalism generally does not. For example, we find market controls often inappropriate for both academic leadership and general higher education. We reject institutional accreditation as the fundamental control mechanism for any function except general higher education. We advocate a different mix of market, government, and academic mechanisms, depending on which type of higher education is under consideration and thus which kind of quality should be promoted.

The big picture is that a better future for higher education in Latin America, so important for a better future for Latin America overall, requires major reform in policy regarding quality control, incentives, and subsidization, among other concerns. A better future in fact requires multiple reforms because no one plan could work for any entire system. These reforms should include significant elements that are prominent in the neoliberal agenda. But most elements in the neoliberal agenda should be modified or qualified substantially and reforms should be applied selectively, according to functions and other variables. Furthermore, reforms must go beyond what the neoliberal agenda features to include not only fresh ideas but also adaptations of the diverse successful reforms that countries have undertaken to date.

To pursue appropriate and sustainable change, reformers must overcome the myths—both positive and negative—about higher education in Latin America. We need to identify what is done reasonably well and what is done poorly. We recommend building on the successes and, in an attempt to achieve more radical change, pursuing policy based on an appreciation of the diversity in the higher education system.

REFERENCES

Adler, Emanuel. 1987. *The Power of Ideology: The Quest for Technological Autonomy in Argentina and Brazil.* Berkeley: University of California.

Albornoz, Orlando. 1979. *Teoría y praxis de la educación superior venezolana.* Caracas: Universidad Central de Venezuela.

———. 1996. "La reinvención de la universidad: Los conflictos y dilemas de la gobernabilidad en América Latina y el Caribe." In Salvador Malo and Samuel Morley, eds., *La educación superior en Latinoamérica: Testimonios de un seminario de rectores.* Washington, D.C.: Inter-American Development Bank.

Albrecht, Douglas, and Adrian Ziderman. 1992. *Funding Mechanisms for Higher Education: Financing for Stability, Efficiency and Responsiveness.* Discussion Book. Washington, D.C.: World Bank.

Altbach, Philip, ed., 1991. *International Encyclopedia of Comparative Higher Education.* New York: Garland.

Altbach, Philip. 1996. *The International Academic Profession: Portraits of Fourteen Countries.* Princeton: The Carnegie Foundation for the Advancement of Teaching.

———. 1999. *Private Prometheus: Private Higher Education in the 21st Century.* Westport, CT: Greenwood.

Alvarez, Benjamin, and Hernando Gómez, eds. 1994. *Laying the Foundation: The Institutions of Knowledge in Developing Countries.* Ottawa: International Development Research Center.

Arregui, Patricia. 1994. "La situación de las universidades peruanas." *Notas para el debate* 12: 9–38.

Asociación Nacional de Universidades e Instituciones de Educación Superior (ANUIES). 1998. *Esquema básico para estudios de egresados.* Mexico City: ANUIES.

Atria, Raúl, et al. 1972. *La universidad latinoamericana: Enfoques tipológicos.* Santiago: Corporation for University Promotion.

Ayarza, Hernán. 1995. "Programas de doctorado en Argentina, Brasil y Chile." In Juan Eduardo Esquivel, ed., *La universidad: Papel y perspectivas del posgrado latinoamericano.* Mexico City: National Autonomous University of Mexico.

Balán, Jorge, ed. 1999. *Politicas de reforma en la educacion superior y la universidad latinoamericana hacia el final de milenio.* Mexico City: UNAM-CRIM.

Balán, Jorge, and Ana García de Fanelli. 1997. "El sector privado de la educación superior." In Rollin Kent, ed., *Los temas críticos de la educación superior en América Latina: Vol. 2. Los años 90. Expansión privada, evaluación y posgrado.* Mexico City: Fondo de Cultura Económica.

Balán, Jorge, and A. Trombetta. 1996. "Una agenda de problemas, políticas y debates sobre educación superior de América Latina." *Perspectivas* 26(1): 419–46.

Belaúnde, Luis Bustamante, and Estuardo Marrou. 1992. *La universidad del Pacífico y las donaciones deducibles: Estudio de un caso.* Lima: Universidad del Pacífico.

Bennell, Paul. 1995. *Using and Abusing Rates of Return: A Critique of the World Bank's 1995 Education Sector Review.* Working Book #22, Institute of Development Studies, University of Sussex, Brighton, United Kingdom.

Berensztein, Sergio. 1995. Untouchables, Fiscal Terrorists, and the Politics of Taxation. Paper presented at the Latin American Studies Association, September 28–30, Washington, D.C.

Birdsall, Nancy. 1996. "Public Spending on Higher Education in Developing Countries: Too Much or Too Little?" *Economics of Education Review* 15(4): 407–419.

Birdsall, Nancy, and Rebecca Foster. 1994. "Lessons from the East." *Hemisfile* 5(4): 6–7.

Borón, Atilio. 1995. La economía política de la educación superior: Reflexiones sobre la experiencia argentina. University of Buenos Aires, Buenos Aires. Mimeo.

Bracho, Teresa, and Jorge Padua. 1995. Características y valor económico de la educación y la formación especializada en el empleo. Center for Economic Research and Teaching, Mexico City. Mimeo.

Bracho, Teresa, and Andrés Zamudio. 1994. "Los rendimientos económicos de la escolaridad en México, 1989." *Economía Mexicana* 3(2): 345–77.

Breslin, Megan. 1999. "Planet University." *University Business* 2(1): 29–39.

Brunner, José Joaquín. 1986. "El movimiento estudiantil ha muerto: Nacen los movimientos estudiantiles." In Juan Carlos Tedesco and H.R. Blumenthal, eds., *La juventud universitaria en América Latina.* Caracas: Regional Center for Higher Education in Latin America and the Caribbean.

———. 1990. *Educación superior en América Latina: Cambios y desafíos.* Santiago: Fondo de Cultura Económica.

———. 1991. *Investing in Knowledge: Strengthening the Foundation for Research in Latin America.* Ottawa: International Development Research Center.

———. 1992. "La educación superior en Chile: 1960–1990." In José Joaquín Brunner, Hernán Courard, and Cristián Cox, eds., *Estado, mercado y conocimiento: Políticas y resultados en la educación superior chilena 1960–1990.* Santiago: Colección Foro de la Educación Superior.

———. 1993. "Evaluación y financiamiento de la educación superior en América Latina: Bases para un nuevo contrato." In Hernán Courard, ed., *Políticas comparadas de educación superior en América Latina.* Santiago: Latin American Faculty of Social Science.

———. 1996. "Educación en América Latina durante la década de 1980." In Rollin Kent, ed., *Los temas críticos de la educación superior en América Latina: Vol. 2. Los años 90. Expansión privada, evaluación y posgrado.* Mexico City: Fondo de Cultura Económica.

Brunner, José Jaoqúin, et al. 1995. *Educación superior en América Latina: Una agenda para el año 2000.* Bogotá: Empresa Editorial, Universidad Nacional de Colombia.

Brunner, José Jaoqúin, and Alicia Barrios. 1987. *Inquisición, mercado y filantropía: Ciencias sociales y autoritarismo en Argentina, Brasil, Chile y Uruguay.* Santiago: Latin American Faculty of Social Science.

Brunner, José Joaquín, Hernán Courard, and Cristián Cox, eds. 1992. *Estado, mercado y conocimiento: Políticas y resultados en la educación superior chilena 1960–1990.* Santiago: Colección Foro de la Educación Superior.

Brunner, José Joaquín, and Roberto Martínez Nogueira. 1999. Evaluación preliminar y metodología para la evaluación de impacto. Fondo de Mejoramiento de la Ciudad Universitaria, Buenos Aires. Processed.

Buchert, Lene, and Kenneth King, eds. 1995. *Learning from Experience: Policy and Practice in Aid to Higher Education.* The Hague: Centre for the Study of Higher Education in Developing Countries.

Calderón, Fernando, and Patricia Provoste. 1990. *Autonomía, estabilidad y renovación: Los desafíos de las ciencias sociales en América Latina.* Buenos Aires: Consejo Latinoamericano de Ciencias Sociales.

Carlson, Sam. 1992. *Private Financing of Higher Education in Latin America and the Caribbean.* Regional Studies Program Report No. 18, World Bank, Washington, D.C.

Casalet, Monica, and Rosalba Casas. 1998. *Un diagnóstico sobre la vinculación universidad-empresa.* Mexico City: CONACYT-ANUIES.

Castro, Claudio de Moura. 1970. "O que Faz um Economista." *Revista Brasileira de Economia* 4 (September-December).

———. 1989. "What is Happening in Brazilian Education?" In Edmar L. Bacha and Herbert S. Klein, eds., *Social Change in Brazil 1945–1985: The Incomplete Transition.* Albuquerque: University of New Mexico Press.

Castro, Claudio de Moura, and Martin Carnoy. 1997. "Qué rumbo debe tomar el mejoramiento de la educación en América Latina?" In Claudio de Moura Castro and Martin Carnoy, eds., *La reforma educativa en América Latina.* Washington, D.C.: Inter-American Development Bank.

Castro, Claudio de Moura, and Juan Carlos Navarro. 1999. "Will the Invisible Hand Fix Latin American Private Education?" In Philip Altbach, ed., *Private Prometheus: Private Higher Education in the 21ˢᵗ Century.* Westport, CT: Greenwood.

CEPAL. 1994. *Anuario estadístico de América Latina y el Caribe.* Santiago, Chile: CEPAL.

Clark, Burton. 1977. *Academic Power in Italy: Bureaucracy and Oligarchy in a National University System.* Chicago: University of Chicago Press.

———. 1983. *The Higher Education System: Academic Organization in Cross-national Perspective.* Berkeley: University of California Press.

———. ed. 1985. *The School and the University: An International Perspective.* Berkeley: University of California Press.

———. 1987. *The Academic Profession: National, Disciplinary, and Institutional Settings.* Berkeley: University of California Press.

———. 1993. *The Research Foundations of Graduate Education: Germany, Britain, France, United States, Japan.* Berkeley: University of California Press.

———. 1995. *Places of Inquiry: Research and Advanced Education in Modern Universities.* Berkeley: University of California Press.

———. 1997. "The Modern Integration of Research Activities with Teaching and Learning." *Journal of Higher Education* 68(3): 241–55.

————. 1998. *Creating Entrepreneurial Universities: Organizational Pathways of Transformation.* Oxford: Pergamon Press.

Clark, Burton, and Guy Neave, eds. 1992. 4 vols. *The Encyclopedia of Higher Education.* New York: Pergamon Press.

Cleaves, Peter. 1987. *Professions and the State: The Mexican Case.* Tucson: University of Arizona Press.

Colclough, Christopher. 1995. "Diversifying the Funding of Tertiary Institutions." In Lene Buchert and Kenneth King, eds., *Learning from Experience: Policy and Practice in Aid to Higher Education.* The Hague: Centre for the Study of Higher Education in Developing Countries.

Contreras, Manuel. 1996. "La evolución de las políticas universitarias en Bolivia." In Horst Grebe López, ed., *Educación superior: Contribuciones al debate.* La Paz: Fundación Milenio.

Corporación Promoción Universitaria (CPU). 1986. *Conocimiento, educación superior y desarrollo nacional: El aporte de la Corporación Promoción Universitaria en las décadas 1966–1986.* Santiago: CPU.

————. 1990. *Tendencias de la educación superior: Elementos para un análisis prospectivo.* Santiago: CPU.

Courard, Hernán. 1992. "Los centros de formación técnica." In José Joaquín Brunner, Hernán Courard, and Cristián Cox, eds., *Estado, mercado y conocimiento: Políticas y resultados en la educación superior chilena 1960–1990.* Santiago: Colección Foro de la Educación Superior.

————. ed. 1993. *Políticas comparadas de educación superior en América Latina.* Santiago: Latin American Faculty of Social Science.

Dooner, Patricio, and Iván Lavados, eds. 1979. *La universidad latinoamericana: Visión de una década.* Santiago: CPU.

Drysdale, Robert. 1987. Higher Education in Latin America: Problems, Policies and Institutional Changes. World Bank, Latin America and Caribbean Office, Washington, D.C. Mimeo.

Durham, Eunice, and Simon Schwartzman. 1992. *Avaliação do Ensino Superior.* São Paulo: Editora da Universidade de São Paulo.

Epstein, Leon. 1974. *Governing the University.* San Francisco: Jossey-Bass.

Esquivel, Juan Eduardo. Forthcoming. "Valorización de las maestrías." In Juan Eduardo Esquivel, ed., *Papel y perspectivas del posgrado latinoamericano.* Mexico City: National Autonomous University of Mexico.

Fernández, Jorge Max. 1980. *Sistema educativo dominicano.* Santo Domingo: Instituto Tecnológico de Santo Domingo.

Fortes, Jacqueline, and Larissa Lomnitz. 1991. *La formación del científico en México.* Mexico City: Siglo XXI.

García de Fanelli, Ana M. 1996. *Estudios de posgrado en la Argentina: Alcances y limitaciones de su expansión en las universidades públicas.* CEDES Working Paper No. 114. Buenos Aires: Centro de Estudios de Estado y Sociedad.

————. 1997. *Las nuevas universidades del conurbano bonaerense: Misión, demanda externa y construcción de un mercado académico.* CEDES Working Paper No. 117. Buenos Aires: Centro de Estudios de Estado y Sociedad.

———. 1998. *Gestión de las universidades públicas: La experiencia internacional.* Buenos Aires: Ministerio de Cultura y Educación.

García Guadilla, Carmen. 1996a. *Conocimiento: Educación superior y sociedad en América Latina.* Caracas: Editorial Nueva Sociedad.

———. 1996b. *Situación y principales dinámicas de transformación de la educación superior en América Latina.* Caracas: CRESALC/UNESCO.

Gazmuri, Pedro, ed. 1992. *Educación superior en Chile: Los programas de posgrado y el desarrollo científico.* Santiago: Foro de la Educación Superior.

Geiger, Roger. 1986. *Private Sectors in Higher Education: Structure, Function, and Change in Eight Countries.* Ann Arbor: University of Michigan.

———. 1993. *Research Relevant Knowledge: American Research Universities since World War II.* New York: Oxford University Press.

Gil, Manuel. 1994. *Los rasgos de la diversidad: Un estudio sobre los académicos mexicanos.* Mexico City: National Autonomous University of Mexico.

———. 1998. "Origen, conformación y crisis de los enseñadores mexicanos : Posibilidades y límites de una reforma en curso." In ANUIES, *Tres décadas de políticas del estado en la educación superior.* Mexico City: ANUIES.

Hodges, Betty Bateman. 1993. Higher Education and the State in Costa Rica. Department of Educational Policy and Leadership, University of Kansas, Lawrence. Unpublished dissertation.

INEP. 1997. *Exame nacional de cursos, 1996.* Brasília: Ministry of Education and Culture.

Instituto Universitario Ortega y Gasset. 1998. *La reforma de la universidad pública de Bolivia.* Madrid: Ortega y Gasset University Institute.

Inter-American Development Bank (IDB). 1997. *Higher Education in Latin America and the Caribbean.* EDU Working Paper No. 101, Inter-American Development Bank, Washington, D.C.

———. 1998. *Facing up to Inequality in Latin America.* Washington, D.C.: Inter-American Development Bank.

James, Estelle. 1986. "Cross-Subsidization in Higher Education: Does It Pervert Private Choice and Public Policy?" In Daniel Levy, ed., *Private Education: Studies in Choice and Public Policy.* New York: Oxford University Press.

Johnstone, D. Bruce. 1986. *Sharing the Costs of Higher Education: Student Financial Assistance in the United Kingdom, The Federal Republic of Germany, France, Sweden, and the United States.* New York: The College Board.

———. 1991. "The Costs of Higher Education." In Phillip Altbach, ed., *International Encyclopedia of Comparative Higher Education.* New York: Garland.

———. 1998. The Financing and Management of Higher Education: A Status Report on Worldwide Reforms. Paper presented at UNESCO World Conference on Higher Education, October, Paris.

Jongbloed, Ben, and Don Westerheijden. 1994. "Performance Indicators and Quality Assessment in European Higher Education." In Victor Borden and Trudy Banta, eds., *Using Performance Indicators to Guide Strategic Decision Making.* San Francisco: Jossey-Bass.

Kells, H. R. 1992. *Self-Regulation in Higher Education: A Multi-national Perspective on Collaborative Systems of Quality Assurance and Control.* London: Jessica Kingsley Publishers.

Kent, Rollin, ed. 1996. *Los temas críticos de la educación superior en América Latina: Estudios comparativos.* Mexico City: Fondo de Cultura Económica.

———. ed. 1997. *Los temas críticos de la educación superior en América Latina: Vol. 2. Los años 90. Expansión privada, evaluación y posgrado.* Mexico City: Fondo de Cultura Económica.

———. 1998. Institutional Reform in Mexican Higher Education: Conflict and Renewal in 3 Public Universities. Paper prepared for the Department of Sustainable Development, Education Unit, Inter-American Development Bank, Washington, D.C.

Kirberg, Enrique. 1981. *Los nuevos profesionales.* Guadalajara: Universidad de Guadalajara.

Kohn, Alfie. 1994. "¿Por qué no funcionan los programas de incentivos?" *Universidad Futura* 5: 61–66.

Kovacs, Karen, ed. 1990. *La revolución inconclusa: Las universidades en la década de los ochenta.* Mexico City: Nueva Imagen.

Krauskopf, Manuel. 1993. *La investigación universitaria en Chile: Reflexiones críticas.* Santiago: Corporation for University Promotion.

Lanning, John. 1971. *Academic Culture in the Spanish Colonies.* Port Washington, N.Y.: Kennikat Press (original 1940).

Lavados, Jaime. 1996. "Commentary." In Salvador Malo and Samuel Morley, eds., *La educación superior en Latinoamérica: Testimonios de un seminario de rectores.* Washington, D.C.: Inter-American Development Bank.

Lemaitre, María José, ed. 1990. *La educación superior en Chile: Un sistema en transición.* Santiago: Corporation for University Promotion.

Lemaitre, María José, and Iván Lavados, eds. 1986. *La educación superior en Chile: Riesgos y oportunidades en los '80.* Second edition. Santiago: Corporation for University Promotion.

Letelier, Mario. 1992. *Los estudios de postgrado y el desarrollo universitario en Chile.* Santiago: Corporation for University Promotion.

Levy, Daniel C. 1980. *University and Government in Mexico: Autonomy in an Authoritarian System.* New York: Praeger.

———. 1981. "Comparing Authoritarian Regimes in Latin America: Insights from Higher Education Policy." *Comparative Politics* 14(1): 31–52.

———. 1986. *Higher Education and the State in Latin America: Private Challenges to Public Dominance.* Chicago and London: The University of Chicago Press.

———. 1991. "Student Activism in Latin America: Explaining the Decline." *Higher Education* 22(2).

———. 1992. "Private Institutions of Higher Education." In Burton Clark and Guy Neave, eds., *The Encyclopedia of Higher Education.* New York: Pergamon Press.

———. 1993. "Recent Trends in the Privatization of Latin American Higher Education: Solidification, Breadth, and Vigor." *Higher Education Policy* 6(4): 12–19.

——. 1994. "Mexico: Towards State Supervision?" In Guy Neave and Frans van Vught, eds., *Government and Higher Education Relationships across Three Continents: The Winds of Change*. Oxford: Pergamon Press.

——. 1996a. *Building the Third Sector: Private Research Centers and Nonprofit Development in Latin America*. Pittsburgh: University of Pittsburgh Press.

——. 1996b. "La calidad en las universidades latinoamericanas: Vino viejo en odres nuevos." In Salvador Malo and Samuel Morley, eds., *La educación superior en Latinoamérica: Testimonios de un seminario de rectores*. Washington, D.C.: Inter-American Development Bank.

——. 1997. "Latin America and the Change in Change: An Increased Role for Institutional Leadership." In Madeleine Green, ed., *Transforming Higher Education: Views from Leaders around the World*. Washington, D.C.: American Council on Education, Oryx Press.

——. 1998a. "Fitting In? Making Higher Education Part of the New Development Model." *Mexican Studies/Estudios Mexicanos* 12(2): 407–40.

——. 1998b. "Internationalised Reform: Overlapping Agendas in East Asian and Latin American Higher Education." *Minerva* 36(4): 367–79.

——. 1999a. "Modernización y democracia en la política de la educación superior." In Jorge Balán, ed., *Políticas de reforma en la educación superior y la universidad latinoamericana hacia el final de milenio*. Mexico City: UNAM-CRIM.

——. 1999b. "When Private Higher Education Does Not Bring Organizational Diversity: Argentina, China, Hungary." In Philip Attbach, ed., *International Encyclopedia of Comparative Education*. New York: Garland.

Lomnitz, Larissa, Leticia Mayer, and Martha Rees. 1983. "Recruiting Technical Elites." *Human Organization* 42: 23–29.

Lorey, David E. 1993. *The University System and Economic Development in Mexico since 1929*. Stanford, CA: Stanford University Press.

Lovera, Alberto, ed. 1994. *Reconversión universitaria*. Caracas: Fondo Editorial Trópykos, Fundación Gual y España, Fondo Editorial APUCV/IPP.

Lucio, Ricardo. 1997. "Políticas de posgrado en América Latina." In Rollin Kent, ed., *Los temas críticos de la educación superior en América Latina: Vol. 2. Los años 90. Expansión privada, evaluación y posgrado*. Mexico City: Fondo de Cultura Económica.

Maassen, Peter, and Frans van Vught. 1994. "Alternative Models of Governmental Steering in Higher Education: An Analysis of Steering Models and Policy-Instruments in Five Countries." In L.C.J. Goedegebuure and Frans van Vught, eds., *Comparative Policy Studies in Higher Education*. Utrecht, Netherlands: Lemma.

Magalhães Castro, Maria Helena. 1995. A Revolução Silenciosa: Autonomia Financeira da USP e UNICAMP. Department of Sustainable Development, Education Unit, Inter-American Development Bank, Washington, D.C. Mimeo.

Magalhães Castro, Maria Helena, and Jean-Jacques Paul. 1992. *As Atividades Profissionais dos Ex-alunos da USP*. NUPES Working Paper. São Paulo: Núcleo de Pesquisas Sobre Ensino Superior da Universidade de São Paulo.

Maier, Joseph, and Richard Weatherhead, eds. 1979. *The Latin American University*. Albuquerque: University of New Mexico.

Malo, Salvador, and Arturo Velázquez, eds. 1998. *La calidad en la educación superior en México: Una comparación internacional.* Mexico City: Miguel Angel Porrua and National Autonomous University of Mexico.

Martínez, Felipe. 1997. "La calidad de la educación superior mexicana y su evaluación." In Sylvia Ortega and David Lorey, eds., *Crisis y cambio de la educación superior en México.* Mexico City: National Autonomous University of Mexico.

Mayorga, Román. 1997. *Cerrando la brecha.* SOC Working Paper No. 101, Inter-American Development Bank, Washington, D.C.

Meek, Lynn, et al., eds. 1996. *The Mockers and the Mocked.* Oxford: Pergamon Press.

Mignone, Emilio. 1992. *Universidad Nacional de Luján: Origen y evolución.* Luján, Argentina: Editorial de la Universidad Nacional de Luján.

Mollis, Marcela. 1990. *Universidades y estado nacional: Argentina y Japón, 1885–1930.* Buenos Aires: Editorial Biblos.

———. 1995. Estado, universidades y gestión de políticas científico-tecnológicas en Argentina: Un estudio de casos. Department of Sustainable Development, Education Unit, Inter-American Development Bank, Washington, D.C.

Moodie, Graeme C. 1986. "Fit for What?" In Graeme C. Moodie, ed., *Standards and Criteria in Higher Education.* Surrey: Guilford.

Muñoz Izquierdo, Carlos, et al. 1995. "Valoración del desarrollo de habilidades cognoscitivas en la educación superior." *Revista Latinoamericana de Estudios Educativos* 25(2): 9–55.

Muñoz Izquierdo, Carlos, and Rosa María Lira Meza. 1990. "Capital cultural, dinámica económica y desarrollo de ia microempresa en la Ciudad de México." *Revista Latinoamericana de Estudios Educativos* 20(4).

Muñoz, Simón. 1996. "Commentary." In Salvador Malo and Samuel Morley, eds., *La educación superior en Latinoamérica: Testimonios de un seminario de rectores.* Washington, D.C.: Inter-American Development Bank.

Neave, Guy. 1988. "On the Cultivation of Quality, Efficiency and Enterprise: An Overview of Recent Trends in Higher Education in Western Europe." *European Journal of Education* 23(1–2): 7–23.

———. 1994. "Government and Higher Education in Developing Countries: A Conceptual Framework." In Guy Neave and Frans van Vught, eds., *Prometheus Bound: the Changing Relationship between Government and Higher Education in Western Europe.* Oxford: Pergamon Press.

Neave, Guy, and Frans van Vught, eds. 1991. *Prometheus Bound: the Changing Relationship between Government and Higher Education in Western Europe.* Oxford: Pergamon Press.

Organisation for Economic Co-operation and Development (OECD). 1993a. *From Higher Education to Employment: Synthesis Report.* Paris: OECD.

———. 1993b. *The Transitions from Elite to Mass Higher Education.* Sydney: OECD.

———. 1998a. *Redefining Tertiary Education.* Paris: OECD.

———. 1998b. Thematic Review of the First Years of Tertiary Education: Country Note, Portugal. OECD, Paris. Processed.

Ornelas, Carlos. 1996. "Evaluación y conflicto en las universidades públicas mexicanas." *Reforma y Utopía* 15: 5–34.

Orozco, Luis Enrique. 1994. Acreditación institucional y calidad de la educación superior en Colombia. Masters Program in Educational Administration, University of the Andes, Bogotá, Colombia. Mimeo.

Patrinos, Harry. 1995. "The Private Origins of Public Higher Education in Greece." *Journal of Modern Greek Studies* 13: 179–200.

Paul, Jean-Jacques. 1997. *O Mercado de Trabalho para os Egressos do Ensino Superior de Fortaleza.* NUPES Working Paper. São Paulo: Núcleo de Pesquisas Sobre Ensino Superior da Universidade de São Paulo.

Persico, Pablo, ed. 1992. *Educación superior chilena: Gestión y administración institucional.* Santiago: Foro de la Educación Superior.

Psacharopoulos, George. 1980. *Higher Education in Developing Countries: A Cost-Benefit Analysis.* Staff Working Book #440, World Bank, Washington, D.C.

———. 1988. "Efficiency and Equity in Greek Higher Education." *Minerva* 26(2): 119–37.

Puryear, Jeffrey. 1982. "Higher Education, Development Assistance, and Repressive Regimes." *Studies in Comparative International Development* 17(2).

———. 1994. *Thinking Politics: Intellectuals and Democracy in Chile: 1973–1988.* Baltimore: Johns Hopkins University Press.

Safford, Frank. 1976. *The Ideal of the Practical: Colombia's Struggle to Form a Technical Elite.* Austin: University of Texas.

Salmi, Jamil, and Adriaan Verspoor, eds. 1994. *Revitalizing Higher Education.* Oxford: Pergamon Press.

Sampaio, Helena. 1998. *O Ensino Superior Privado: Tendências da Última Década.* NUPES Working Paper. São Paulo: Núcleo de Pesquisas Sobre Ensino Superior da Universidade de São Paulo.

Scherz, Luis, ed. 1975. *La universidad latinoamericana en la década del 80: Proyecciones del desarrollo en América Latina y su incidencia en la educación superior.* Santiago: Corporation for University Promotion.

Schiefelbein, Ernesto. 1985. "Latin America." In Burton Clark, ed., *The School and the University: An International Perspective.* Berkeley: University of California Press.

———. 1996. "El financiamiento de la educación superior en América Latina." In Salvador Malo and Samuel Morley, eds., *La educación superior en Latinoamérica: Testimonios de un seminario de rectores.* Washington, D.C.: Inter-American Development Bank.

Schwartzman, Simon. 1991. *A Space for Science: the Development of the Scientific Community in Brazil.* University Park: Pennsylvania State University Press.

———. 1996a. *América Latina: Universidades en transición.* Washington, D.C.: Organization of American States.

———. 1996b. "Las universidades latinoamericanas en contexto." In Salvador Malo and Samuel Morley, eds., *La educación superior en Latinoamérica: Testimonios de un seminario de rectores.* Washington, D.C.: Inter-American Development Bank.

————. 1998. *Higher Education in Brazil: The Stakeholders.* LCSHD Paper Series No. 28. Washington, D.C.: World Bank.

Serrano, Sol. 1993. *Universidad y nación: Chile en el siglo XIX.* Santiago: Editorial Universitaria.

Steger, Hanns-Albert. 1979. "The European Background." In Joseph Maier and Richard Weatherhead, eds., *The Latin American University.* Albuquerque: University of New Mexico.

Taquini, Jr., Alberto C. 1972. *Nuevas universidades para un nuevo país.* Buenos Aires: Editorial Estrada.

Task Force on Higher Education, Latin American Studies Association. 1994. "Higher Education amid the Political-Economic Changes of the 1990s." *LASA Forum* 24(1): 3–15.

Tedesco, Juan Carlos. 1983. *Tendencias y perspectivas en el desarrollo de la educación superior en la América Latina y el Caribe.* Paris: United Nations Educational, Scientific, and Cultural Organization.

————. ed. 1992. *Posgrado y desarrollo en América Latina.* Mexico: Union of Latin American Universities.

Trow, Martin. 1974. "Problems in the Transition from Elite to Mass Higher Education." In OECD, ed., *Policies for Higher Education.* Paris: Organization for Economic Cooperation and Development.

Tunnermann, Carlos. 1996. *La educación superior en el umbral del siglo XXI.* Caracas: UNESCO/CRESALC.

Tyler, Lewis, et al. 1997. *Higher Education in Latin America.* New York: Garland Press.

UNESCO. 1995. *Documento de política para el cambio y el desarrollo en la educación superior.* Paris: United Nations Educational, Scientific, and Cultural Organization.

Urquiola, Miguel. 1993. *El sistema de financiamiento de la educación superior universitaria en Bolivia.* UDAPSO Working Paper. La Paz: Analysis Unit on Social Policy.

Valenti, Giovanna, et al. 1997. *Los egresados de la UAM en el mercado de trabajo: Investigación evaluativa sobre la calidad de la oferta de servicios educativos.* Mexico City: National Autonomous University of Mexico.

Vessuri, Hebe. 1993. *La evaluación académica: Enfoques y experiencias.* Paris: CRESALC/UNESCO.

————. 1997. "A 'House for Solomon' in the Caribbean: The Venezuelan Institute of Scientific Research." *Science, Technology & Society* 2(1): 41–71.

Winkler, Donald. 1990. *Higher Education in Latin America. Issues of Efficiency and Equity.* World Bank Discussion Paper. Washington, D.C.: World Bank.

Wolff, Lawrence, and Douglas Albrecht, eds. 1992. *Higher Education Reform in Chile, Brazil, and Venezuela.* Washington, D.C.: World Bank.

World Bank. 1994. *Higher Education: The Lessons of Experience.* Washington, D.C.: World Bank.

————. 1995. *Priorities and Strategies for Education: A World Bank Sector Review.* Washington, D.C.: World Bank.